Assessing Speaking

THE CAMBRIDGE LANGUAGE ASSESSMENT SERIES

Series editors: J. Charles Alderson and Lyle F. Bachman

In this series:

Assessing Speaking

Sari Luoma

CAMBRIDGE
UNIVERSITY PRESS

CAMBRIDGE UNIVERSITY PRESS
Cambridge, New York, Melbourne, Madrid, Cape Town, Singapore, São Paulo, Delhi

Cambridge University Press
The Edinburgh Building, Cambridge CB2 8RU, UK

www.cambridge.org
Information on this title: www.cambridge.org/9780521804875

© Cambridge University Press 2004

This publication is in copyright. Subject to statutory exception
and to the provisions of relevant collective licensing agreements,
no reproduction of any part may take place without the written
permission of Cambridge University Press.

First published 2004
4th printing 2008

Printed in the United Kingdom at the University Press, Cambridge

A catalogue record for this publication is available from the British Library

ISBN 978-0-521-80487-5 paperback

To my parents, Eila and Yrjö Luoma
Thank you for your support and for your faith in me

Contents

Series editors' preface to *Assessing Speaking*

The ability to speak in a foreign language is at the very heart of what it means to be able to use a foreign language. Our personality, our self image, our knowledge of the world and our ability to reason and express our thoughts are all reflected in our spoken performance in a foreign language. Although an ability to read a language is often the limited goal of many learners, it is rare indeed for the teaching of a foreign language not to involve learners and teachers in using the language in class. Being able to speak to friends, colleagues, visitors and even strangers, in their language or in a language which both speakers can understand, is surely the goal of very many learners. Yet speaking in a foreign language is very difficult and competence in speaking takes a long time to develop. To speak in a foreign language learners must master the sound system of the language, have almost instant access to appropriate vocabulary and be able to put words together intelligibly with minimal hesitation. In addition, they must also understand what is being said to them, and be able to respond appropriately to maintain amicable relations or to achieve their communicative goals. Because speaking is done in real-time, learners' abilities to plan, process and produce the foreign language are taxed greatly. For that reason, the structure of speech is quite different from that of the written language, where users have time to plan, edit and correct what they produce. Yet teachers often focus narrowly on the development of grammatically accurate speech which may conflict with a learner's desire to communicate and be understood.

Speaking is also the most difficult language skill to assess reliably. A person's speaking ability is usually judged during a face-to-face interaction, in real time, between an interlocutor and a candidate. The assessor has to make instantaneous judgements about a range of aspects of what is being said, as it is being said. This means that the assessment might depend not only upon which particular features of speech (e.g. pronunciation, accuracy, fluency) the interlocutor pays attention to at any point in time, but upon a host of other factors such as the language level, gender, and status of the interlocutor, his or her familiarity to the candidate and the personal characteristics of the interlocutor and candidate. Moreover, the nature of the interaction, the sorts of tasks that are presented to the candidate, the questions asked, the topics broached, and the opportunities that are provided to show his or her ability to speak in a foreign language will all have an impact on the candidate's performance. In addition to all the factors that may affect performance, the criteria used to assess the performance can vary enormously, from global assessments to detailed analytic scales. The ways in which these scales are interpreted by an assessor, who may or may not be the same person as the interlocutor, are bound to have an impact on the score or scores that the candidate is ultimately awarded. There are, of course, ways of overcoming or at least addressing some of these problems, by careful construction of the tasks used to elicit speech, by careful training of both assessors and interlocutors, through audio or video recording of the speech event and by allowing assessors time to review and revise their judgements. Assessing speaking is thus not impossible, but it is difficult.

The strongest feature of this book is that Sari Luoma discusses with great clarity the problems of assessing speaking, and she does this in the light of her broad and deep understanding of the nature of speaking. Drawing upon a wide base of research and theory, she synthesises a large literature into a very readable overview of what is involved in speaking in a second or foreign language. Her down-to-earth approach will appeal both to language teachers who want to assess their students' ability to speak in a foreign language and to researchers of speaking and language assessment.

In this book, as in other volumes in the series, applied linguistic theory and research are drawn upon in order to enhance our understanding of the nature of what is to be tested and assessed. In addition, research into language testing is examined for what it can tell us about the most appropriate ways of assessing speaking, and for insights it can offer into the nature of this central aspect of language use. Although this book is grounded in research and theory, it is highly practical and is aimed at those who need to develop assessments of speaking ability. It thus offers insights and advice that will broaden the repertoire of readers, give greater understanding of the issues involved, and lead to practical solutions to knotty problems.

Sari Luoma has wide experience of test development in a range of different contexts, and of research into test development and test validation, particularly in the assessment of speaking. She has taught testing and assessment to a range of students and practitioners, which has clearly informed both the content and the style of this volume. We are confident that readers will both learn from, and enjoy, this book.

J. Charles Alderson
Lyle F. Bachman

Acknowledgements

I am grateful to Charles Alderson and Lyle Bachman, the series editors, for the efforts they put into helping me finish this book. They applied a successful balance of pressure and support in the course of a long writing process with many ups and downs. The insightful comments I received about the content and structure of the book, especially during the revision stage, improved the quality of the text considerably.

I also want to thank some friends and colleagues who have read the manuscript in its various stages and offered valuable advice. Annie Brown's frequent and frank comments on the second-last version helped me restructure several chapters. Bill Eilfort, Mika Hoffman and Ari Huhta also gave their time, advice and support. Furthermore, I want to acknowledge the helpful comments of two groups of Egyptian teachers of English, too many to name individually, who participated in an Advanced Course on Language Testing at the University of California Santa Cruz Extension in the late summer and early fall of 2002. We used an early version of the manuscript as course material, and their comments and groans made me change my writing style and encouraged me to introduce more examples. I want to thank Jean Turner for inviting me to join the teaching group for the two courses.

I must also thank the teachers and colleagues who discussed their speaking assessment practices with me and allowed me to use their specifications and tasks as examples in the book: Tarmo Ahvenainen, Janna Fox, Angela Hasselgren, and Paula Niittyniemi-Mehn.

Finally, I want to thank the editors at Cambridge University Press,

Mickey Bonin and Alison Sharpe, for their help in getting the book ready for publication. Whatever faults that remain in the book are mine.

The author and publishers are grateful to those authors, publishers and others who have given permission for the use of copyright material identified in the text.

Speech samples in *Teaching Talk: Strategies for production and assessment* (1984) by G. Brown, A. H. Anderson, R. Shillcock and G. Yule, Cambridge University Press.

Speech samples in *Exploring Spoken English* (1997) by R. Carter and M. McCarthy, Cambridge University Press.

Finnish National Foreign Language Certificate: National certificates scale, National Board of Education, Helsinki.

ACTFL Proficiency Guidelines – Speaking (Revised 1999) © American Council on the Teaching of Foreign Languages.

Materials selected from *TSE ® and SPEAK ® Score User Guide* (2001). Reprinted by permission of Educational Testing Service, the copyright owner. However, the test questions and any other testing information are provided in their entirety by Cambridge University Press. No endorsement of this publication by Educational Testing Service should be inferred.

Table 4.5 *Common European Framework* (pages 28–29), Table 3. Common Reference Levels: qualitative aspects of spoken language use; in Schneider, G. and North, B. (2000) *Fremdsprachen können – was heisst das?:* 145; a further development from North, B. (1991) "*Standardisation of Continuous Assessment Grades*" in Language Testing in the 1990s; Alderson, J.C. and North, B. 1991, London, Macmillan/ British Council: 167–178.1. © Council of Europe.

Table 4.6 "*Common European Framework*" (page 79), Goal-oriented co-operation. © Council of Europe.

Melbourne Papers in Language Testing (2001) by E. Grove and A. Brown.

Understanding and Developing Language Tests by C. Weir, © Pearson Education Limited.

Fluency scale by A. Hasselgren from *Testing the Spoken English of Young Norwegians,* to be published in 2004 by Cambridge University Press © UCLES.

Table 4.8: Hierarchy of processing procedures by M. Pienemann in *Language Processing & Second Language Development-Processability Theory.* John Benjamins Publishing Co., Amsterdam/Philadelphia 1998.

Writing English Language Tests (4th ed) by J. B. Heaton, Longman © Pearson Education Limited.

Examples of Tasks (1997), by the Nasjonalt Laeremiddelsenter, Norway.

Interaction outline for a pair task, and task card for two examinees in a paired interview, University of Cambridge Local Examinations Syndicate ESOL.

Testing material by Paula Niittyniemi-Mehn, Virtain Yläaste, Finland.

Examinee's test booklet in a tape-based test, 'Violence in Society as a group project work sheet' and a reading exercise, © CAEL 2000 (Canadian Academic English Language Assessment).

Testing procedures by Tarmo Ahvenainen, Kymenlaakso Polytechnic, Finland.

Sample Test in English by M-Riitta Luukka, Centre for Applied Language Studies, University of Jyväskylä, Jyväskylä 2003.

Phone pass practice test © Ordinate Corporation.

CHAPTER ONE

Introduction

Speaking skills are an important part of the curriculum in language teaching, and this makes them an important object of assessment as well. Assessing speaking is challenging, however, because there are so many factors that influence our impression of how well someone can speak a language, and because we expect test scores to be accurate, just and appropriate for our purpose. This is a tall order, and in different contexts teachers and testers have tried to achieve all this through a range of different procedures. Let us consider some scenarios of testing speaking.

> Scenario 1
> *There are two examinees and two testers in the testing room. Both examinees have four pictures in front of them, and they are constructing a story together. At the end of their story, one of the testers asks them a few questions and then closes the discussion off, says goodbye to the examinees, and stops the tape recorder. After the examinees leave, the testers quickly mark their assessments on a form and then have a brief discussion about the strongest and weakest features of each performance. One examinee had a strong accent but was talkative and used quite a broad range of vocabulary; the other was not as talkative, but very accurate. They are both given the same score.*

This is the oral part of a communicative language assessment battery, mostly taken by young people who have been learning a foreign language at school and possibly taking extra classes as one of their hobbies. The certificates are meant to provide fairly generic proof of level of achievement. They are not required by any school as such, but those who have them are exempted from initial language courses at several universities and vocational colleges. This may partly explain why the test is popular among young people.

Scenario 2

The language laboratory is filled with the sound of twelve people talking at the same time. A few of them stop speaking, and soon the rest follow suit. During the silence, all the examinees are looking at their booklets and listening to a voice on their headphones. Some make notes in their booklets; others stare straight ahead and concentrate. Then they start again. Their voices go up and down; some make gestures with their hands. The examinees' turns come to an end again and another task-giving section begins in their headphones. The test supervisor follows the progress of the session at the front of the room. At the end of the session, the examinees leave the lab and the supervisor collects back the test booklets and starts the transfer of performances from the booths to the central system.

To enable the test session in Scenario 2 to run as expected, many steps of planning, preparation and training were required. The starting point was a definition of test purpose, after which the developers specified what they want to test and created tasks and assessment criteria to test it. A range of tasks were scripted and recorded, and a test tape was compiled with instructions, tasks, and pauses for answering. The test was then trialled to check that the tasks work and the response times are appropriate. The rating procedures were also tested. Since the system for administering the test was already set up, the test was then introduced to the public. The scores are used, among other things, to grant licenses to immigrating professionals to practise their profession in their new country.

Scenario 3

Four students are sitting in a supposed office of a paper mill. Two of them are acting as hosts, and the two others are guests. One of the hosts is explaining about the history of the factory and its present production. The teacher pops in and observes the interaction for a couple of minutes and then makes a quiet exit without disrupting the presentation. The guests ask a few questions, and the speaker explains some more. At the end, all four students get up and walk into the school workshop to observe the production process. The other host takes over and explains how the paper machine works. There is quite a lot of noise in the workshop; the speaker almost has to shout. At the end of the tour, the speaker asks if the guests have any more questions and, since they do not, the hosts wish the guests goodbye. The students then fill in self-assessment and peer assessment sheets. The following week's lesson is spent reflecting on and discussing the simulations and the peer and self-assessments.

This assessment activity helps vocational college students learn factory presentation skills in English. The task is a fairly realistic simulation of one of their possible future tasks in the workplace. The assessment is an integrated part of other learning activities in class, in that the class starts preparing for it together by discussing the properties of a good factory tour, and they use another couple of lessons for planning the tours and practising the presentations. Working in groups makes efficient use of class time, and having students rate themselves and their peers further supports student reflection of what makes a good factory tour. Pair work in preparing the presentation simulates support from colleagues in a workplace. The teacher's main role during the preparation stage is to structure the activities and support the students' work. During the assessment event he circulates among the groups and observes each pair for a couple of minutes, and after the event he evaluates performances, conducts assessment discussions with each pair, and makes notes on their peer and self-assessments for future use in grading.

Scenario 4
The interviewer and the examinee are talking about the examinee's job. The interviewer asks her to compare her present tasks to her earlier job, and then to talk about what she would like to do in the future. And what if she were to move abroad? This is obviously not the first time the examinee is talking about her work in English, she has a very good command of the specialist vocabulary, and while her speaking rate is not very fast, this may be how she speaks her mother tongue, too. She has no problem answering any of the interviewer's questions. In around fifteen minutes, the interviewer winds down the discussion and says goodbye to the examinee. She has made an initial assessment of the performance during the interview, and now she makes a final evaluation and writes it down on an assessment form. Then she has a quick cup of coffee, after which she invites the next examinee into the room.

The test in Scenario 4 is part of a proficiency test battery for adults. **Proficiency tests** are examinations that are not related to particular learning courses but, rather, they are based on an independent definition of language ability. This particular test is intended for adults who want a certificate about their language skills either for themselves or for their employers. Talking about their profession and their future plans is thus a relevant task for the participants. The certificates that the examinees get report a separate score for speaking.

The surface simplicity of the individual interview as a format for testing speaking hides a complex set of design, planning and training that underlies the interaction. This is especially true if the interview is part of a proficiency test, but it is also true in settings where the participants may know each other, such as interview tests conducted by a teacher. This is because, like all tests, the interview should be fair to all participants and give them an equal opportunity to show their skills. Since the test is given individually, the interviewer needs to follow some kind of an outline to make sure that he or she acts the same way with all the examinees. If some of the tests are conducted by a different interviewer, the outline is all the more important. Furthermore, the criteria that are used to evaluate the performances must be planned together with the interview outline to ensure that all performances can be rated fairly according to the criteria. This partly depends on the interlocutor's interviewing skills, and in big testing organisations interviewer training and monitoring are an essential part of the testing activities. The interviewers in the test of Scenario 4 are trained on a two-part workshop and then conduct a number of practice interviews before being certified for their job.

The cycle of assessing speaking

As the examples above show, assessing speaking is a process with many stages. At each stage, people act and interact to produce something for the next stage. While the assessment developers are the key players in the speaking assessment cycle, the examinees, interlocutors, raters and score users also have a role to play in the activities. This book is about the stages in the cycle of assessing speaking and about ways of making them work well. It is meant for teachers and researchers who are interested in reflecting on their speaking assessment practices and developing them further.

A simplified graph of the activity cycle of assessing speaking is shown in Figure 1.1. The activities begin at the top of the figure, when someone realises that there is a need for a speaking assessment. This leads to a planning and development stage during which, in a shorter or longer process, the developers define exactly what it is that needs to be assessed, and then develop, try out and revise tasks, rating criteria and administration procedures that implement this intention. They also set up quality assurance procedures to help them monitor everything that happens in the assessment cycle. The assessment can then begin to be used.

Figure 1.1 The activity cycle of assessing speaking

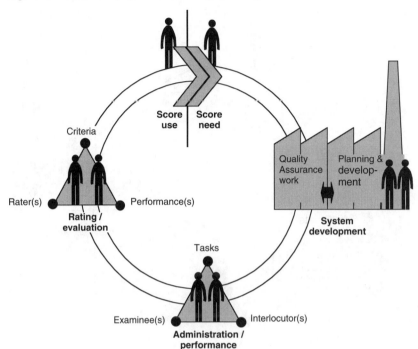

The cycle continues with two interactive processes that are needed for 'doing' speaking assessment. The first is the test administration/test performance process, where the participants interact with each other and/or with the examiner(s) to show a sample of their speaking skills. This is often recorded on audio- or videotape. The second process is rating/evaluation, where raters apply the rating criteria to the test performances. This produces the scores, which should satisfy the need that was identified when the test development first started. I use the term **score** in a broad sense to refer to numerical scores, verbal feedback, or both. At the end of the cycle, if the need still exists and there is a new group of examinees waiting to be assessed, the cycle can begin again. If information from the previous round indicates some need for revision, this has to be done, but if not the next step is administering a new round of tests.

Figure 1.1 is simplified in many senses, two of which are that, while it shows activity stages, it does not show the products that are taken forward from each stage or the scope of the quality assurance work in the cycle. Before going into these, let me say something about the shapes

Figure 1.2 Stages, activities and products in assessing speaking

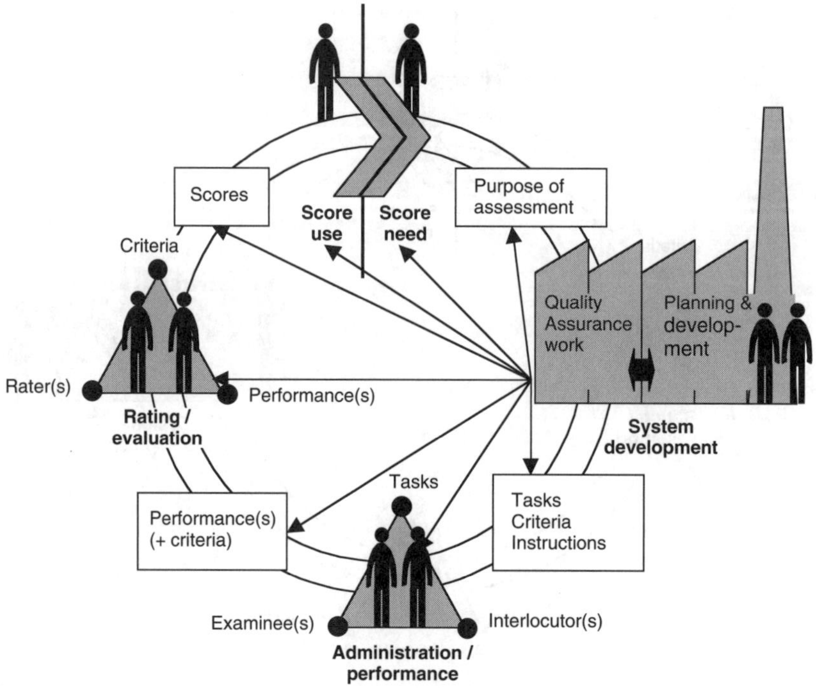

used for the stages. At the top of the cycle, score need and score use are indicated by dovetailed arrows. This signifies the need for the start and end of the cycle of assessing speaking to fit together. The second stage is shown as a factory. This is the test developers' workplace. They develop the assessment and produce the documents that are needed (tasks, criteria, instructions) to guide the activities. As at any factory, quality assurance is an important aspect of the development work. It ensures that the testing practices being developed are good enough for the original purpose. Moving along the cycle, the administration and rating processes are shown as triangles because each of them is a three-way interaction. The human figures in the cycle remind us that none of the stages is mechanical; they are all based on the actions of people. Score need and score use bind the stages of assessing speaking into an interactive cycle between people, processes and products.

Figure 1.2 shows the same activity cycle with the most important products – documents, recordings, scores, etc. – and the scope of the quality assurance work drawn in. To begin from the top of the figure, the first document to be written after the realisation that speaking scores are needed is a clarification of the purpose of the assessment. This guides all the rest of the activities in the cycle. Moving along, the main products of the planning stage are the tasks, assessment criteria, and instructions to participants, administrators, interlocutors and assessors for putting the assessment into action. At the next stage, the administration of the test produces examinee performances, which are then rated to produce the scores.

As is clearly visible in Figure 1.2, quality assurance work extends over the whole assessment cycle. The main qualities that the developers need to work on are construct validity and reliability. **Construct** is a technical term we use for the thing we are trying to assess. In speaking assessments, the construct refers to the particular kind of speaking that is assessed in the test. Work on **construct validity** means ensuring that the right thing is being assessed, and it is the most important quality in all assessments. Validation work covers the processes and products of all the stages in the speaking assessment cycle. They are evaluated against the definition of the speaking skills that the developers intended to assess. **Reliability** means making sure that the test gives consistent and dependable results. I will discuss this in more detail in Chapter 8.

The organisation of this book

This chapter has given a brief introduction into the world of assessing speaking. The next four chapters deal with existing research that can help the development of speaking assessments. Chapter 2 summarises applied linguistic perspectives on the nature of the speaking skill and considers the implications for assessing the right construct, speaking. Chapter 3 discusses task design and task-related research and practice. Chapter 4 takes up the topic of speaking scales. It introduces concepts related to scales in the light of examples and discusses methods of scale development. Chapter 5 discusses the use of theoretical models as conceptual frameworks that can guide the definition of the construct of speaking for different speaking assessments.

Chapters 6 through 8 then provide practical examples and advice to support speaking test development. Chapter 6 presents the concept of test specifications and discusses three examples. Chapter 7 concentrates on exemplifying different kinds of speaking tasks and discussing their development. Chapter 8 focuses on procedures for ensuring the reliability and validity of speaking assessments. The main themes of the book are revisited in the course of the discussion. The chapter concludes with a look at future directions in speaking assessment.

In this chapter, I have introduced the activity of assessing speaking. Different assessment procedures for speaking can look very different, they may involve one or more examinees and one or more testers, the rating may be done during the testing or afterwards based on a recording, and the scores may be used for a wide range of purposes. Despite the differences, the development and use of different speaking assessments follow a very similar course, which can be modelled as an activity cycle. The activities begin with the developers defining the purpose of the assessment and the kind of speaking that needs to be assessed, or the test construct. To do this, they need to understand what speaking is like as a skill. This is the topic of the next chapter.

CHAPTER TWO

The nature of speaking

In this chapter, I will present the way speaking is discussed in applied linguistics. I will cover linguistic descriptions of spoken language, speaking as interaction, and speaking as a social and situation-based activity. All these perspectives see speaking as an integral part of people's daily lives. Together, they help assessment developers form a clear understanding of what it means to be able to speak a language and then transfer this understanding to the design of tasks and rating criteria. The more these concrete features of tests are geared towards the special features of speaking, the more certain it is that the results will indicate what they purport to indicate, namely the ability to *speak* a language.

Describing spoken language

What is special about spoken language? What kind of language is used in spoken interaction? What does this imply for the design of speaking assessments?

The sound of speech

When people hear someone speak, they pay attention to what the speaker sounds like almost automatically. On the basis of what they hear, they make some tentative and possibly subconscious judgements about the speaker's personality, attitudes, home region and native/non-native speaker status. As speakers, consciously or unconsciously, people use their speech to create an image of themselves to others. By using speed and pausing, and variations in pitch, volume and intonation, they also create a texture for their talk that supports and enhances what they are saying. The sound of people's speech is meaningful, and that is why this is important for assessing speaking.

The sound of speech is a thorny issue for language assessment, however. This is first of all because people tend to judge native/non-native speaker status on the basis of pronunciation. This easily leads to the idea that the standard against which learner pronunciation should be judged is the speech of a native speaker. But is the standard justified? And if it is not, how can an alternative standard be defined?

The native speaker standard for foreign language pronunciation is questioned on two main accounts (see e.g. Brown and Yule, 1983: 26–27; Morley, 1991: 498–501). Firstly, in today's world, it is difficult to determine which single standard would suffice as *the* native speaker standard for any language, particularly so for widely used languages. All languages have different regional varieties and often regional standards as well. The standards are valued in different ways in different regions and for different purposes, and this makes it difficult to choose a particular standard for an assessment or to require that learners should try to approximate to one standard only. Secondly, as research into learner language has progressed, it has become clear that, although vast numbers of language learners learn to pronounce in a fully comprehensible and efficient manner, very few learners are capable of achieving a native-like standard in all respects. If native-like speech is made the criterion, most language learners will 'fail' even if they are fully functional in normal communicative situations. Communicative effectiveness, which is based on comprehensibility and probably guided by native speaker standards but defined in terms of realistic learner achievement, is a better standard for learner pronunciation.

There are, furthermore, several social and psychological reasons why many learners may not even *want* to be mistaken for native speakers of a language (see e.g. Leather and James, 1996; Pennington and Richards, 1986): a characteristic accent can be a part of a learner's identity, they may not want to sound pretentious especially in front of their peers, they may want recognition for their ability to have learned the language so well despite their non-native status, and/or they may want a means to convey their non-native status so that if they make any cultural or politeness mistakes, the listeners could give them the benefit of the doubt because of their background.

Pronunciation or, more broadly, the sound of speech, can refer to many features of the speech stream, such as individual sounds, pitch, volume, speed, pausing, stress and intonation. An important question is whether all of these can be covered under one rating criterion. Moreover, should the focus be on accuracy of pronunciation or expressiveness of the speaker's use of voice, or both? The solutions depend on the purpose for which the scores will be used and the importance of the sound of speech for that purpose. If there are many other rating criteria besides pronunciation, fitting accuracy and effectiveness into a criterion like 'naturalness of pronunciation' may be the only option. If the sound of speech is a main focus in the assessment, evaluating aspects of it separately gives material for more detailed feedback.

A focus on pronunciation accuracy is attractive because it can be judged against a norm and, even if the norm is not easy to define given the discussion above, gross deviations from it are easy enough to notice. Since accuracy is related to comprehensibility, it is often at least one aspect of a pronunciation criterion, but comprehensibility is much more than accuracy. It often includes speed, intonation, stress and rhythm, all of which may be more important for the overall comprehensibility of the talk than the accuracy of individual sounds. If the emphasis in the assessment is on ability to create meaning in discourse, the developers might want to evaluate 'interactional efficiency'. This would encompass the examinees' use of stress and intonation to highlight important phrases, or to suggest in what particular way (e.g. ironically) their words should be interpreted. In yet other contexts, they might want to focus on 'expressiveness' as indicated by the general texture of the talk, the speaker's use of speed and pausing, and variations in pitch, tone and volume. This might be especially relevant in tasks such as creative storytelling or certain kinds of role plays, where liveliness of expression is a central element in task performance. Thus, in designing assessment criteria, the developers need to consider the type of information about the sound of speech that they need. They also have to make sure that their tasks give enough material for rating these features, and that they develop the criteria that serve their needs.

Spoken grammar

Both first and second language learners' progress is often tracked according to the grammatical forms that they can produce accurately (see e.g. Larsen-Freeman and Long, 1991: 38–41 for a discussion on this point). In general, learners are seen to proceed from knowing a few structures to knowing more and more, from using simple structures to using more complex ones, and from making many errors to making few if any at all. Learner grammar is handy for judging proficiency because it is easy to detect in speech and writing, and because the fully fledged grammars of most languages are well known and available for use as performance standards. However, the grammar that is evaluated in assessing speaking should be specifically related to the grammar of speech.

Written sentences, spoken idea units

A major difference between speech and writing is that speakers do not usually speak in sentences. Rather, speech can be considered to consist of **idea units**, which are short phrases and clauses connected with *and*, *or*, *but* or *that*, or not joined by conjunctions at all but simply spoken next to each other, with possibly a short pause between them. The grammar of these strings of idea units is simpler than that of the written language with its long sentences and dependent and subordinate clauses. This is because speakers are trying to communicate ideas that listeners need to comprehend in real time, as they are being spoken, and this means working within the parameters of the speakers' and listeners' working memory. Idea units are therefore usually about two seconds or about seven words long, or shorter (Chafe, 1985). The units are usually spoken with a coherent intonation contour, and they are often limited on both sides by pauses or hesitation markers. Many idea units are clauses with a verb phrase, a noun phrase and a prepositional phrase, but some of them do not contain a verb, and sometimes an idea unit is started by one speaker and completed by another.

Grammar in planned and unplanned speech

There are of course some situations where complex grammatical features and a high degree of written language influence are not only common but also expected and highly valued. Examples of this include speeches, lectures, conference presentations, and expert discussions where speakers represent their institution or their profession. These situations involve **planned speech** (Ochs, 1979), where the speakers have prepared and possibly rehearsed their presentations in advance, or they express well-thought-out points and opinions, which they may have voiced many times before. **Unplanned speech**, in contrast, is spoken on the spur of the moment, often in reaction to other speakers. It is particularly in unplanned speech that short idea units and 'incomplete sentences' are common, although even in planned speech, idea units are usually shorter than in writing, because the speakers know that their talk has to be understood by listeners in real time.

The concepts of planned and unplanned speech are closely connected to another factor that affects the grammar of speech, namely the level of formality of the speaking situation. Situations that involve planned speech tend to be relatively formal, whereas unplanned speech situations can range from formal to informal. Formal situations require more written-like language with more complex grammar, whereas informal situations call for more oral-like language with strings of short phrases and short turns between speakers.

For assessing speaking, it is in fact useful to see the differences between spoken-like and written-like language as a continuum, with highly oral language at one end and highly literate language at the other (Tannen, 1982). In addition to grammar, oral and literate speech differ in their pronunciation and choice of vocabulary, among other things. Test designers can design tasks for various places on the oracy–literacy continuum by varying things like planning time and the kinds of speaker roles and role relationships that they include in the tasks.

Two examples

To illustrate the nature of grammar in speech, let us look at two examples of transcribed talk. The first comes from Brown *et al.* (1984). A young British postgraduate is describing what happened when she ordered a snack from room service in an American hotel. The second word, *er*, is a voiced hesitation sound, which could also be spelled *eh* or *uh*. A single plus sign indicates a short pause and two plus signs a longer pause. The speaker is being interviewed by a researcher to give material for a study. In other words, the speakers are relative strangers and the speaking situation is fairly formal.

> and + er + I was pretty exhausted and I phoned up room service and said that I wanted a sandwich + + nothing's ever straightforward in America (laugh) – 'what kind of sandwich' + + I said 'well' er + hummed and hawed +

and he said 'well + there's a list in your drawer' + 'in your chest of drawers' + + so I had a look at it and gawd there was everything (laugh) you know + and I saw roast beef + so I phoned back and said I would have a roast beef sandwich (laugh) + and a glass of milk + so an hour later + + nothing happened you see + so I phoned him up again and yes + they were coming + and in walked this guy with a tray + an enormous tray and a steel covered + plate + dinner plate you see + so I lifted that up + and I've never seen anything like it + + + there was three slices of bread lying on this plate + and there was I counted eight slices of roast beef + hot roast beef + with gravy and three scoops of mashed potato round the outside + an enormous glass of milk and a glass of water

(Brown *et al.*, 1984: 17)

Brown *et al.* point out that this is a very competent storyteller who structures long turns confidently. Even so, the chunks of language are mostly clause-sized, they are strung together with the conjunction *and* or follow one another without conjunctions, and the vocabulary is rather simple. There are short phrases, pauses, repetitions and reformulations. On two occasions, the speaker does not follow number concord. A non-native speaker in a test situation might be marked down for such a performance. Similarly, the shortness of phrases and the absence of 'advanced' vocabulary might affect the rating. Yet this is a natural sample of native speaker storytelling.

The second example is from unplanned and informal dialogue. Three British female students (S01–S03) are chatting in the kitchen of a house they are renting.

1 <S01> Does anyone want a chocolate or anything?
2 <S02> Oh yeah yes please
3 <S03> Yes please
4 <S02> [laughs]
5 <S03> [laughs]
6 <S01> You can have either a Mars Bar, Kit-Kat or erm cherry Bakewell
7 <S03> Oh erm it's a toss-up between [<S02> [laughs]] the cherry
8   Bakewell and the Mars Bar isn't it?
9 <S01> Well shall I bring some in then cos you might want another one
10   cos I don't want them all, I'm gonna be
11 <S03> Miss paranoid about weight aren't you?
12 <S01> Yes but you know

13 <S03>   You're not fat Mand
14 <S01>   I will be if I'm not careful
15 <S02>   Oh God
. . .

(Carter and McCarthy, 1997: 85)

This is typical casual talk. Most of the turns consist of one short meaning unit and speakers change quickly. In her longest turn, Student 1 uses the causal connector *cos* (lines 9 and 10) and, at the last juncture, simple stringing along. Other than that, the coherence in the discourse is created by thematic linking. On line 11, Student 3 shortens her turn by omitting the subject and the verb, *you are*, but her meaning is still fully comprehensible. The use of phrases like *you know* and *it's . . . isn't it* make the turns characteristically spoken-like and informal.

The internal structure of idea units

Many spoken idea units are clauses, grammatically speaking, but the way that idea units are structured is often slightly different from standard written clauses. Two structures that clearly belong to spoken-like language use are **topicalisation** and **tails**.

Topicalisation, or thematic fronting, gives special informational emphasis to the initial element of a clause in informal speech, as in *Joe, his name is* (Quirk and Greenbaum, 1976). Topicalisation breaks the standard word order of written language. In speaking, the word order does not seem 'broken' in any sense, however, since the aim is to emphasise the topic. It is a very frequent feature of informal talk, and McCarthy and Carter (1995: 211) suggest that the explanation is that it has significant interpersonal meaning. It often indicates that an important topic of conversation is to follow. Thus, their example of *That house in the corner, is that where you live?* is presumably an introduction into a discussion on the house or the neighbourhood, something that the speaker is reminded of upon seeing the house.

Tails, in turn, are noun phrases that come at the end of a clause. In a way they are the mirror image of topicalisation, in that they repeat a pronoun that has been used earlier in the clause. By using tails, speakers can emphasise the comment they make at the beginning of the clause, and still make it clear what they are talking about, as in *It's very nice, that road through Skipton to the Dales* (McCarthy and Carter, 1995). The comment that the speaker expresses at the beginning of the clause is often an evaluation, such as *he's quite a comic, that fellow, you know*, but not always, as in *'cos otherwise they tend to go cold, don't they, pasta*. Tails emphasise the point made at the beginning of the clause, and at the same time, they create an informal tone in the talk.

Both topicalisation and tails follow clear patterns, which can be formed into 'rules' for talk. The patterns are characteristically spoken-like, but not traditionally taught in language classes or talked about in grammars. They create an impression of naturalness and interpersonal involvement in spoken discourse, and if examinees use them appropriately they could be rewarded for it. However, they cannot be punished for not using them, because they are not obligatory in any context.

To summarise the discussion on spoken grammar, speech is organised into short idea units, which are linked together by thematic connections and repetition as well as syntactic connectors. The most frequent connectors are coordinating conjunctions (*and, or, but*, etc.). Some speaking situations call for more literate grammar with complete clauses and subordination. These are typically formal speaking situations, which may involve prepared talk such as a presentation.

Speakers may emphasise points by topicalisation, which means starting their turn with the main topic and making the word order unusual, or tails, which means using the natural emphasis of the beginning of their turn for a comment or an evaluation and putting the noun that they are making their comment on at the end of the clause. This gives talk a spoken flavour. It adds interpersonal and evaluative tones, which is typical for spoken discourse.

Words, words, spoken words

Many rating scales for speaking include descriptions of vocabulary use, and at the highest levels these often talk about being able to express oneself precisely and providing evidence of the richness of one's lexicon. This can indeed be important in professional contexts or when trying to convey detailed information. Well-chosen phrases can also make descriptions or stories vivid, and learners who can evoke the listener's feelings deserve to be credited for their ability. However, very 'simple' and 'ordinary' words are also very common in normal spoken discourse, and using these naturally in speech is likewise a marker of highly advanced speaking skills (see e.g. Read, 2000). Moreover, there is a core of phrases and expressions that are highly typical for speaking, which contribute to the listener's impression of the speaker's fluency. They work at the inter-personal level by keeping the conversation going and developing the rela-tionship between the speakers. This aspect of word use should also be rewarded in assessing speaking.

Specific and generic words

Some forms of written language require the use of specific words to make it clear what is being talked about. For example, a written instruction for how to adjust an office chair states: *Use the ball adjustment to move the lumbar support to a position where it supports the back.* If the same instruction were given orally in a hypothetical set of video-taped instruc-tions, similar words might well be used, but with added visual support. In an interactive speaking situation, the same instructions would probably sound quite different. The speakers would use many generic words such as *this one / that one, the round thing, move, put, fine,* and *good.* The instruction-giver and the chair-user would probably exchange several turns to make sure that the task got done properly.

Generic words are very common in spoken interaction. Even though they are not precise, they are fully comprehensible in the speaking situa-tion because they talk about people, things or activities that can be seen or because they are familiar to the speakers. They make spoken commu-nication quick and easy, and few people would find anything strange about this in their mother tongue. Generic words may also come naturally to second-language learners, but in a foreign language context where learners have few opportunities to speak the language outside the class-room this feature of spoken language may be harder to notice and learn. Assessment designers can help this by including descriptions of effective use of generic words in rating scales. This sends the message to learners and raters that generic words are important for the naturalness of talk.

Another common feature of interactive and relatively informal talk is the use of vague words like *thing, thingy, thingummy* and *whatsit* when the speaker cannot think of the word he or she needs to use. Channell (1994) has investigated the use of these words in English, but she refers to other researchers' examples for French and presumes that all languages have a set of such words. Vague words help the speaker go on regardless of the missing word, and at the same time they appeal to the listener to understand and supply it if they can. They are natural in informal talk, and if learners use them appropriately they deserve to be rewarded for it.

Fixed phrases, fillers and hesitation markers

Speakers also need to know words, phrases and strategies for creating time to speak. These are sometimes called fillers or hesitation markers, and they include expressions such as *ah, you see, kind of, sort of,* and *you know,* as well as whole expressions such as *That's a good question,* or *Now let me see.* Speakers often also use repetition of their own words, or of those used by the previous speaker, to achieve the same purpose, i.e. to keep the floor while formulating what they want to say. These expressions are very common in native speaker speech, but for some reason their appearance in test performances by foreign language learners is sometimes frowned upon. When writing assessment scales, test developers should perhaps consider if examinees who manage to use such expressions successfully in a test situation should be rewarded for it instead.

Fixed conventional phrases are also used for other purposes in talk than creating time. Examples of these include responses like *I thought you'd never ask* or *I'm doing all right, all things considered.* The phrases either always have the same form, or they constitute a formula where one or two slots can be filled by various terms (e.g. *What a nice thing to say, What a horrible thing to say*). They have been called lexicalised sentence stems by Pawley and Syder (1983), and lexical phrases by Nattinger and DeCarrico (1992). They are easy for speakers to use because they come almost automatically when a relevant situation arises and because, once a speaker begins such a phrase, saying it will give them time to judge the situation, perhaps plan how they want to put what they want to say next, or think of something else to say.

Word use in studies of assessing speaking

There are a few studies that support the relevance of the above-mentioned characteristics of speech for assessing speaking. Towell *et al.* (1996), for instance, show that learners' use of lexical phrases is connected with a listener's experience of the speaker's fluency. That is, if two learners use an approximately similar lexicon in their speech, but one of them also uses a range of fixed phrases while the other does not, the one who uses the phrases is perceived to be the more fluent of the two. And if a learner uses a wide range of fixed phrases, listeners tend to interpret that as proof of a higher level of ability than when a learner is using a few stock phrases in all kinds of contexts.

Hasselgren (1998) investigated learners' use of filler words with three groups of speakers: British native speaker schoolchildren of 14–15 years of age, and two ability groups of Norwegian schoolchildren of the same age, high and low. Hasselgren called the verbal phenomenon she investigated **'smallwords'**, which she defined as 'small words and phrases, occurring with high frequency in the spoken language, that help to keep our speech flowing, yet do not contribute essentially to the message itself' (p. 4). Her results support the case that the more smallwords a learner uses, the better their perceived fluency.

Nikula's (1996) study of a range of similar expressions, which she considered under the heading of 'pragmatic force modifiers', adds the observation that even advanced learners produce a much narrower range of 'spoken-like' expressions and discourse markers than native speakers. She studied the speech habits of her non-native speakers also in their mother tongue, and was thus able to prove that the difference was not caused by personal or cultural communication style but was truly related to language ability. Together, these studies strongly support the case that the use of spoken-like words is important in speaking performance.

Slips and errors

Normal speech contains a fair number of slips and errors such as mispronounced words, mixed sounds, and wrong words due to inattention. If the listeners notice, they tend to pardon native speakers because they believe them to 'know', but in the speech of second or foreign language learners slips and errors mysteriously acquire special significance. Their slips can signal lack of knowledge, and this seems to be important for many listeners. While there are some errors that only learners make, such as using *no* + verb to express negation in English (*I no write*) or violating simple word order rules, there are others that are typical for all speakers. Assessment designers may have to provide special training to raters to help them outgrow a possible tendency to count each 'error' that they hear.

Processing and reciprocity

Bygate (1987) summarises the above features of spoken language use by contrasting them with writing. He suggests that the differences can be explained with reference to two sets of conditions: processing and reciprocity. Processing conditions are connected with time, the crucial difference being that, while writers can generally take as much time as they need to produce their text and readers can pace their reading (on a separate occasion) to their needs and interests, the processes of speaking and listening are most often intertwined and happen under the pressure of ever ticking time. The solution to this is reciprocity, by which Bygate means that speakers react to each other and take turns to produce the text of their speech together. This helps the speakers with the processing demands of speech, but it also has a social dimension in that their phrases and turn-taking patterns create and reflect the social relationship between them.

Speaking as meaningful interaction

Speaking and spoken interaction

Teaching and testing experts often talk about speaking as a technical term to refer to one of the various skills that language learners should develop and have. This type of speaking tends to be seen as something that *individuals* do. It is legitimate, and for educational purposes useful, to see speaking in this way too, because it is true that individuals speak, and an important part of language use is personal. Nevertheless, it is also important to remember that speaking forms a part of the shared social activity of talking.

In a typical spoken interaction, two or more people talk to each other about things that they think are mutually interesting and relevant in the situation. Their aim can be to pass the time, amuse each other, share opinions or get something done, or they can aim to do several of these and other things at once. The point in their interaction is that they do these things together. Each participant is both a speaker and a listener; they construct the event together and share the right to influence the outcomes – which can be both shared and individual.

The openness of meanings in interaction

When people talk and listen to each other, they are driven by a quest for meaning, but meanings are not always clear and explicit. Moreover, people know that anything that is said has not just one meaning but many: it says something about some topic or other, but it also indicates the speaker's attitude towards the topic and towards the other participant(s) and reflects the speaker's knowledge about the history of the topic, his or her views about what might be happening next, and more. As discussed earlier in this chapter, this kind of non-explicitness appears in many verbal forms, and it has many motivations.

The openness of meanings is not only a convenience in speech; it is also an effective strategy for speakers. They can avoid committing themselves to a statement or attempt to find out how the listener feels about the topic before proceeding. They can try to find out what the listener already knows, what he or she is prepared to accept or understand, and what the best strategy might be to persuade the listener to accept their point of view. For example, someone may introduce the topic of going to the movies and listen for reactions before raising the idea that this group of people might want to go out to a particular show that weekend. A member of the group who has other commitments may then say that she likes the idea but does not know yet because something urgent may come up with work or something. This is strategically a highly skilful way of using language, and speakers, at least in a language that they live in, use vague expressions for these purposes automatically, because they are a fundamental part of spoken communication.

Language learners' attempts at vagueness may cause peculiarities in discussions. They may simply sound strange because they do not know how interpretations are appropriately left open. Alternatively, they may use the right kind of strategies, but the listener may fail or refuse to recognise their intention. The natural appearance of open meanings in a discussion involving a learner is a clear sign of highly advanced speaking skills, as it proves that the learner is able to produce successful indirect utterances and that the listener is willing and able to interpret and act upon this in the context of the interaction. This kind of naturalness may not be easy for raters to notice unless their attention is specifically drawn to it through training, rater instructions and wordings of assessment scales.

Variation within spoken language use

Although spoken language as a whole can be contrasted with written language, there is also a lot of systematic variation within spoken language use. The analysis of this is a part of discourse analysis, which is a vast area of research in applied linguistics. A thorough introduction to the field is not attempted here (for this, see e.g. Schiffrin, 1994; McCarthy and Carter, 1997). In the sections below, I discuss three significant areas in spoken discourse for assessing speaking: purposes of talk, the speaking situation and speaker roles. They help assessment developers think about what *kinds* of talk need to be included in their assessment, and thus focus the assessment on the right construct.

Talking to chat and talking to inform

One way in which speech events differ from each other is the purpose for which the people are talking to each other. With this approach to analysing talk, Brown *et al.* (1984) characterise two extremes: chatting or listener-related talk, and information-related talk. They stress that this is not a clear-cut dichotomy but rather a dimension along which sections of talk will be situated. Moreover, both types of talk can occur in one and the same speech event; in fact, this is what normally happens. Information-related talk often comes sandwiched between social chat, and a social chat can easily turn into a serious discussion.

Brown *et al.* (1984) define **chatting** as the exchange of amicable conversational turns with another speaker. The primary purpose is to make and maintain social contact, to oil the social wheels, and thus chatting forms a large part of anyone's social life. Skilful chatting involves finding a fluid stream of topics that the speakers find sufficiently interesting to take up, and on which they can find a shared angle. The topics are not necessarily discussed very deeply, and it is more important to create a positive atmosphere and to agree than to express oneself precisely or to be completely truthful. Chatting in one's first language can only really become strenuous on a social rather than linguistic dimension. However, we are not all equally socially gifted, and not all equally good at chatting. Yet, as Brown *et al.* point out, chatting in the first language is so closely connected to personality and individual communication styles that it cannot really be taught.

In language teaching, however, some focus on at least the basic phrases for chatting is necessary, and when chatting occurs it involves the learners' personalities and their social behaviour. It also involves their culture, as appropriate topics for chatting differ between cultures. This causes some difficult dilemmas for assessing speaking.

If the assessment situation involves chatting in the target language, as it often does during the initial and final stages of the interaction and maybe in other stages as well, the developers have to consider how far it is necessary or justified to assess a learner's personality or social skills. It is perhaps realistic to accept that it is impossible to exclude the social aspects of personality from the assessment completely, but it may be possible to avoid highlighting some sociability aspects of chatting. One way in which this is attempted in many tests is by telling raters not to assess the initial stages of a test interaction. In some assessments, however, chatting might be the main focus of assessment, especially in learning contexts if it has been taught recently. Then it would be important to make sure that the participants know what kind of talk they should aim for to do well on the test.

The other end of Brown *et al.*'s (1984) dimension of kinds of talk, **information-related talk**, refers to speech aimed at transferring information on a particular topic. People's talk at work mostly belongs to this end of the continuum, for example policemen talking to witnesses, nurses and doctors talking to patients and to each other, or factory workers interacting with each other. Information-related talk is also very much a part of teaching–learning situations, and these kinds of tasks are very often included in assessment situations as well. As with chatting, Brown *et al.* make the point that native speakers vary in their ability to produce information-related talk, but in contrast to chatting they feel that the techniques for more effective information-related talk can be taught.

The most important point about information-related talk is getting the message across and confirming that the listener has understood it. Establishing common ground, giving the information in bite-sized chunks, logical progression, questions, repetitions and comprehension checks help speakers reach this aim. These features should therefore appear in examinee performances on information-related tasks, and they may help explain why some of them do better on the test than others. Once the developers analyse some learner performances to find out exactly how the performances at different ability levels differ, for example whether weaker performers fail to establish common ground or do not sequence the information logically, they can use these concepts in rating scales to indicate how raters can tell performances at different levels apart.

Apart from basic information-structuring skills, information-related talk also requires other skills for organising communication and making it easy to follow. Brown and Yule (1983) discuss five types of information-oriented tasks for language learning, including telling a story from pictures. In this task, speakers need to be able to identify the main characters and refer to them consistently, describe the main events and activities, and mention any significant changes in characters, time or locations. Stories become more difficult to tell the more characters there are who are difficult to tell apart, so that a story involving three girls is more difficult than one involving two girls, which in turn is more difficult than a story involving a girl and a boy. They also become more difficult the more events there are, and the more changes in characters, time or locations that the story involves. Good storytelling routines are important for speakers, as one of the most common types of chatting involves personal stories about accidents or embarrassing situations (Rintell, 1990; Jones, 2001). To be able to convey the nature of the situation and the speaker's emotions, learners need to have routinised the basic storytelling skills discussed above. I will return to information-related tasks and task difficulty in Chapter 3.

Talking in different social situations

One set of features that has an influence on what gets said in a speech event and how it is said is the social and situational context in which the talk happens. Hymes (1972) has helpfully summarised these concerns into a framework that forms the acronym SPEAKING. The framework has so many categories because it is meant to be applicable to a large variety of social situations, but all of them may not be relevant for every situation.

The SPEAKING framework lists the potential social and contextual factors influencing speech as:

Situation	The physical setting (for instance a classroom) and the nature of the event (for instance an end-of-term test of speaking).
Participants	Speaker, hearer, audience, etc.; for instance, two examinees, an interlocutor and an assessor (whether present in the situation or absent, only listening to the interaction afterwards from tape).

Ends	Conventional outcomes of the event, if any. For instance, accomplishing whatever task is the goal of the event, or producing a test score and verbal feedback. The ends also include the individual participants' goals, such as exposing the strengths and weaknesses of the examinees' speaking ability, showing one's ability to speak a foreign language at its best, or making fair and equitable assessments.
Act sequence	The form and content of speech acts: the content of what is said, and the way it is said; how each act is spoken, and the sequence of acts in the discourse.
Key	Tone, manner, or spirit of act; for instance, supportive, friendly, open, formal, impersonal, tentative, withdrawn.
Instrumentalities	Channel or mode, e.g. spoken, written, pre-recorded. Forms of speech: dialects, accents, and varieties used.
Norms	Norms of interpretation and norms of interaction, such as right/responsibility to initiate topics, ask questions, express views, ask for clarification, explain, elaborate.
Genre	Categories such as a joke, lecture, description, instruction, storytelling, presentation.

Assessment developers can use this framework when they make initial plans for their test. It will help them describe the test construct in some detail. Later in the development work, the framework can guide the comparison of individual test administrations against each other, which is important for fairness. If there are clear differences, the scores may not be comparable. The categories can be used to compare talk in the test with speaking situations that the examinees are likely to meet outside the test. This is significant because the assessment developers probably want to predict the examinees' ability to cope with the non-test situations on the basis of their test results. If there are differences, the predictions may not be safe.

The importance of any differences is a value judgement, however. Hymes's framework can make the analysis of the differences more systematic, and thus help make this judgement more informed. The key questions that the assessment developers have to answer are: is there a difference, is it important given the purposes of this assessment, and what are the alternatives to the current tasks and rating criteria?

Two particularly interesting variables in the SPEAKING framework are Key and Norms. Brown and Lumley (1997), for example, investigated a role-play task between examiners and test takers where the examiners played the patients and the test takers played their professional role as health workers. Their evidence indicated that although the examiners received instructions about how to act, they nevertheless behaved differently in the test situation, some being more 'difficult' as patients and others more supportive. This had the effect that the test was more difficult for some test takers than others. Brown and Lumley propose specially focused examiner training as a solution. I do not know of similar analyses of role-plays between two test takers, and this might be an interesting area to look into. Other task types could also be analysed. Furthermore, it seems possible that norms of interaction and interpretation might have an influence on test discourse. Test takers, examiners and raters may also use different norms when performing their roles in the testing process. It would be interesting to know how this influences the process and outcomes of language tests.

Roles, role relationships and politeness

Another feature that influences speakers' choice of words in interaction is speaker roles and role relationships. Together with the social and contextual features of the speaking situation, they can particularly be seen in the way that politeness appears in the talk. Politeness is usually the reason why people do not communicate 'maximally efficiently', as they would if they followed Grice's (1975) four conversational maxims:

- quantity: give sufficient information but not too much;
- quality: say only what you know to be true;
- relation: be relevant;
- manner: be brief, clear and orderly.

People can, for instance, talk 'too much' because they want to seem interested and thus polite, or they may bend the truth in order not to hurt someone. The features of role relationships that influence politeness and directness are the relative power of the speaker over the hearer, relative rights and obligations to initiate something or to follow and agree to the other's initiation, the social distance between the speaker and hearer, and the degree to which something to be said is regarded as an imposition (i.e. a significant request) in the situational and cultural context (Thomas, 1995). For a discussion on politeness, see Thomas for a concise introduction, and Brown and Levinson (1987) for more extensive discussion.

Impressions of politeness are almost guaranteed to influence the assessment of spoken performances, whether acknowledged or not. Politeness is a difficult concept for assessment, however, because it is guided by principles rather than laws. If an examinee uses a phrase that a rater perceives to be impolite, how much more polite should he or she have been in order to have avoided making that impression? There are no clear rules about exactly what he or she should have said. Moreover, politeness is difficult for assessment also because it is interpersonal and social, and the social relationship between test participants is artificial. A solution might be to give politeness assessments in gross terms only, for instance on the three levels of *appropriate, somewhat appropriate* and *questionable or worse.*

Conclusion

In this chapter, I have discussed speaking as meaningful interaction between people. Some applied linguistic analyses, especially ones that focus on linguistic features, may at first sight seem to emphasise form at the cost of meaning, but in fact the concepts that are used in them are closely related to meaning as well. Comprehensibility of pronunciation is a case in point. For those who are new to speaking assessment, the most important point to remember from the linguistic description of spoken language is the special nature of spoken grammar and spoken vocabulary. This is especially important in creating rating criteria. Regarding interactive and social features of speaking, few people would question their relevance for understanding what speaking is like. From our own experience with speaking, we know that conversations with different people turn out to be different even if we ourselves have more or less the same things to say, because speakers react to each other and construct discussions together. We know that speakers' meanings are vague and that we vary the way we speak according to the situation. But how should this affect the speaking assessments that we design? I suggest that there are at least two implications. Firstly, we must analyse the kind of speaking that we need to assess in a particular assessment context in terms of social and situational needs. Secondly, we must remember that speaking is interactive when we design rating criteria and procedures, and reward examinees when they repeat or mirror the other speaker's phrases and structures or develop topics by referring to earlier turns and building on them, because this shows that they know how to work interactively with other speakers.

The aim in all assessments is to focus on the right thing. This provides the basis for construct validity. Thus, the developers of speaking assessments must have a clear understanding of what speaking is like and then:

- define the kind of speaking they want to test in a particular context;
- develop tasks and rating criteria that test this;
- inform the examinees about what they test;
- and make sure that the testing and rating processes actually follow the stated plans.

In the rest of the book, I will discuss and provide examples of how this can be done. The next chapter begins the journey by discussing speaking tasks.

CHAPTER THREE

Speaking tasks

When we are assessing speaking, we guide the examinees' talk by the tasks that we give them. These outline the content and general format of the talk to be assessed and they also provide the context for it. As we saw in the previous chapter, language use varies by purpose and context, so task design is a very important element in developing assessments.

Task design begins with the needs of the assessment situation, as pointed out in Chapter 1. The purpose of the test and the practical circumstances in which it will be arranged set the general guidelines, but the most important factor when designing tasks is the construct-related information that the scores must deliver, or in other words what the score users need to know about the examinees' speaking skills. This dictates the types of skills that the tasks should make the examinees show. In learning-related assessment, this is often guided by what has been taught recently, but end-of-course tests may need to provide more general information about the examinees' skills, more or less like formal, external examinations. Existing research on speaking tasks can help task design. In this chapter, I will summarise the current state of this research.

Furthermore, to put their speaking tasks into practice, assessment designers need to create not only the tasks but also the instructions to be given to the examinees, the task materials such as pictures or role-play cards that will be needed, and the instructions to interlocutors that will be used. In the second half of the chapter, I will summarise advice from language-learning and language-testing research for creating these. The chapter finishes with a summary. I will begin, however, by defining two basic terms.

Defining 'context' and 'task'

Context

Context is one of the central concepts of language use. It is usually defined broadly, covering the linguistic, physical, psychological and social dimensions of the situation in which language is used. Hymes's (1972) SPEAKING framework, as discussed towards the end of Chapter 2, presents one well-known way of dividing context into dimensions that can be analysed.

In practice, **context** refers to everything in the speaking situation except the talk that is being produced at a particular moment. Thus, it includes concrete aspects of the situation such as the place where the talk happens, and cognitive and experiential aspects such as the language-use experiences that the speakers bring to the situation and the goals they have in a particular conversation.

Context guides what is said in a speaking situation, and by manipulating the features of context through task properties, assessment designers can direct the talk on their test. However, this does not allow them to predict exactly what will be said. This is because speakers are only influenced by those features of the context that are salient to them, and this varies from individual to individual and from situation to situation (Douglas, 1998). Moreover, since the relationship between the speakers, as well as their experience of the speaking situation, also form parts of context, it is simply impossible to engineer all the contextual features of a speaking situation before it actually happens. Nevertheless, some aspects of context can be controlled and their effect on discourse predicted to some extent. This is why teachers, textbook writers and assessment designers pay so much attention to the properties of language-use tasks.

Task

Tasks are activities that people do, and in language-learning contexts tasks are usually defined in terms of language use. Nunan (1993: 59) defines a **communicative task** as:

> . . . a piece of classroom work which involves learners in comprehending, manipulating, producing or interacting in the target language while their attention is principally focused on meaning rather than form. . . . Minimally, a task will consist of some input data and one or

more related activities and procedures. Input refers to the data that learners are to work on: it may be linguistic (e.g. a radio broadcast), non-linguistic (e.g. a set of photographs), or 'hybrid' (e.g. a road map). In addition, tasks will have, either explicitly or implicitly (and in most cases these are implicit), goals, roles of teachers and learners and a setting.

This definition is helpful for test development as well, because it details the elements that the task designer has to design: input, goals, roles and settings.

Bachman and Palmer (1996: 44) have defined language use tasks in very similar terms. To modify their definition slightly for the specific context of speaking, **speaking tasks** can be seen as activities that involve speakers in using language for the purpose of achieving a particular goal or objective in a particular speaking situation. The emphasis in this definition is on goal-oriented language use, and it is appropriate for test tasks as well as events or 'tasks' outside testing situations.

Initial task design

By initial task design, I refer to the first decisions about what the test will be like; what it will contain. This includes plans about the tasks that the speakers will be given and about the practical arrangements for the test. The decisions also concretise the construct to be assessed.

What the speakers are asked to do

One of the key decisions in task design is what the speakers will be asked to *do* with language. In an early study on the nature of talk, Brown and Yule (1983) made distinctions between four different types of informational talk: description, instruction, storytelling and opinion-expressing/justification. Their main point was that each of the types follows its own routines of organising information for easy comprehension, and with practice learners can improve their control of these routines and thus increase their language-use skills. They also suggested that in general the above is the logical order of difficulty between the types, although specific orders would be very difficult to predict once the internal complexity of tasks within the types is taken into account. That is, it is not easy to say how complex a description task needs to be before it becomes more difficult than a simple instruction or story-telling task.

Bygate (1987) made even finer distinctions between types of speaking tasks:

Factually oriented talk	Evaluative talk
• description	• explanation
• narration	• justification
• instruction	• prediction
• comparison	• decision

Like Brown and Yule, he pointed out that speakers' use of language is different in each of these categories. If someone is good at describing, it does not automatically mean that he or she is also good at comparing things, telling a story or justifying an opinion. This means that it is useful to test the types of talk separately, as they may give different information about the learners' skills. If there are alternative versions of a task within a test, it would probably also be useful to keep them within the same talk type, so that all examinees get some kind of a comparison task, for example, rather than some of them getting an instruction task and others a comparison. If tasks in a test are categorised like this, the construct definition is related to types of activity that the examinees are asked to do, and the scores can be used to indicate this.

The categories listed above concern information-related talk. As discussed in Chapter 2, this often comes sandwiched between social chatting, and the two types of talk together make up the test discourse. During task design, however, it is common to focus on the informational aspect of the talk, because it decides the content area and the types of language activities that will be included in the test discourse. Social talk will be included in all kinds of tasks, and because of its effect of oiling the social wheels of communication it will probably influence the assessors' impression of how well the examinees perform the tasks. If desired, assessment criteria may be tuned to pick this up specifically; I will discuss this in the next chapter.

Communicative functions

Another way of looking at what the speakers have to do in speaking tasks is by analysing the actions they perform when they say something. This approach to language use was first introduced by the linguistic philosopher J. L. Austin (1962), who called the actions *speech acts* (for example, *requesting* or *confirming*). His insight that people use utterances to do things as well as to convey information was groundbreaking, and it led to much further work in philosophy of language, sociolinguistics and discourse analysis about the rules that people follow in their linguistic action. Grice's (1975) maxims for speaker collaboration regarding quantity of information, truthfulness, relevance and presentation manner, which were mentioned in Chapter 2, are part of this work.

A similar idea about purposes of language use also underlies the work in language education by van Ek (1975) and Wilkins (1976) on notional/functional syllabuses. The idea was that learners usually need the language that they are learning for some real-life purpose, and so syllabuses could be organised according to what the learners need to be able to do (functions) and the words and phrases needed for the topics that they need to be able to talk about (notions). Putting emphasis on learner needs and language use for real-life purposes was radically different from the grammatically based syllabus that was common in the 1960s and early 1970s, and it paved the way for the arrival of the communicative syllabus in the 1980s. Although the beginnings of the notional/functional syllabus were originally independent from speech act theory, the shared focus on using language to do things made it easier for the language education community to apply work from discourse analysis into classroom contexts (Douglas and Smith, 1997: 10). The combination of both strands can also be seen in the *Common European Framework of Reference* (CEF) (Council of Europe, 2001).

The CEF divides functional competence into two categories: macro and micro. **Macrofunctions** refer to chunks of spoken or written language serving the same functional purpose, such as description, narration, commentary, explanation and demonstration. These are the same as the types of talk discussed by Brown and Yule (1983) and Bygate (1987). **Microfunctions**, in turn, are related to individual actions, which are often completed within a turn in an interaction, such as inviting, apologising or thanking (Council of Europe, 2001: 125). The CEF groups the microfunctions into six main categories:

- giving and asking for factual information, e.g. describing, reporting, asking;
- expressing and asking about attitudes, e.g. agreement/disagreement, knowledge/ignorance, ability, permission;

- suasion, e.g. suggesting, requesting, warning;
- socialising, e.g. attracting attention, addressing, greeting, introducing;
- structuring discourse, e.g. opening, summarising, changing the theme, closing;
- communication repair, e.g. signalling non-understanding, appealing for assistance, paraphrasing.

As learners improve, they learn to do more with words, i.e. they gain control of more microfunctions, but more significantly they learn more ways of expressing the functions they know, so that they can fit their talk to different language use situations. Beginning learners may only know one way of asking for something, for example, while more advanced learners know several. Very advanced language learners can accommodate their talk to the demands of all kinds of situations and express the things they want to do with whatever tones that they want.

Language functions can be an important element in designing speaking assessments. The Test of Spoken English (TSE), a tape-based test brought out by the Educational Testing Service (ETS), uses them as a primary design principle (ETS 2001b: 7). The functions included in each test are describing information that is presented graphically in the test booklet, narrating from visual materials (a picture sequence), summarising, giving directions based on visual materials, giving instructions, recommending, advising or suggesting, giving and supporting an opinion, comparing or contrasting, hypothesising, predicting or speculating, and persuading, apologising or complaining (Douglas and Smith, 1997: 12). The mock examination example of giving and supporting an opinion is:

> 3. One of your favourite movies is playing at the theater. Please tell me
> about the movie and why you like it. (60 seconds)   (ETS, 2000)

The seconds are printed at the end of the prompt because the test is tape-based and the examinees need information about how long they can spend responding to the task. The task continues the theme of the previous one, which asked the examinees to explain the way to the movie theatre on the basis of a map.

The TSE functions seem to be much like the microfunctions in the Council of Europe documents, and they cover a broad range of possible language-use situations. This is indeed the intention of the test developers. While it might be a drawback that the construct is not contextualised in particular situations of language use, the advantage of this approach is that the results can be relevant for several different ones. With formal tests such as the TSE, professional standards require that the developers provide evidence for this relevance for each intended use of the test. In this case, since the TSE is used for selecting candidates for teaching assistantships, among other things, the developers need to show that the functions are relevant for teaching assistants' language use, and that examinees who gain good scores on the test meet the language require ments for their work while those who do not would find the language requirements of the work too demanding. In less formal assessment con- texts, research studies about correspondence of language use in the assessment and outside it are less common, but it would make sense to make the organising principle for the assessment and the teaching cur- riculum coherent. Thus, when functions are an important organising principle in a teaching program, this can also be a good basis for design- ing learning-related assessments of speaking for it.

Individual, pair and group tasks

The most typical way of arranging speaking tests is to assess examinees one at a time, often in an interview format. This became a standard when oral assessment was first introduced in the 1950s, and in the following 30 years the format was not really questioned even though test methods for other skills were criticised and revised. Although individual testing is costly in terms of examiner time, it is flexible in that the questions can be adapted to each examinee's performance, and it gives the testers a lot of control over what happens in the interaction. However, the fact that the interviewer has considerable power over the examinee in an interview has been recognised as one of the central weaknesses of this test type (see e.g. Savignon, 1985; Bachman, 1988; van Lier, 1989; Lazaraton, 1992). The interlocutor initiates all phases of the interaction and asks the questions, whereas the role of the examinee is to comply and answer. In other types of interactions, such as discussions or conversations, the rights and responsibilities of the partici- pants to take the initiative are more balanced, and interviews do not give direct evidence of the examinee's ability to deal with these demands. Yet they do provide the examinees with an opportunity to show a range of how well they can speak the language, so they do work as tests. However, for some purposes, the evidence may need to be broader.

A one-to-one test does not necessarily need to be an unstructured, interlocutor-led interview. It can be structured and contain a number of different tasks. A typical structured interview would begin much like an unstructured one, with a warm-up discussion of a few easy questions such as getting to know each other or talking about the day's events. The main interaction, then, would contain the pre-planned tasks, such as describing or comparing pictures, narrating from a picture series, talking about a pre-announced or examiner-selected topic, or possibly a role-play task or a reverse interview where the examinee asks questions of the interviewer. In some professionally oriented tests, the examinee gives a prepared presentation for which he or she has received instructions in advance, and the presentation is followed by a discussion with the examinee in his or her expert role. In another context, the test might be a discussion of some texts and/or videos that the examinee has read or viewed before the interview. The test would end in a wind-down phase where the aim is to put the examinee at ease.

The choice of tasks for the main part of the test (description, narrative, topic-based discussion, etc.) depends on the kind of information that is needed from the scores. I will discuss examples of structured interview tasks in Chapter 7.

Given the limitations of the individual interview as a test mode, one alternative is to interview pairs. Swain (2001) mentions three arguments in favour of doing this. The first is the wish to include more types of talk than the traditional interview and thus broaden the evidence gathered about the examinees' skills. The second has to do with the relationship between testing and teaching, either in the sense of wishing to influence teaching so as to encourage more pair work in classes, or in the sense of repeating in testing what is happening in teaching already. The third reason is economical, as interviewing pairs reduces the amount of examiner time needed for conducting the tests. The point about paired interviews is that during the main part of the test the examinees are asked to interact with each other, with the examiner observing rather than taking part in the interaction directly.

Paired interviews are used in the five examinations of the Cambridge main suite, for example. These are the Key English Test, the Preliminary English Test, the First Certificate in English, the Certificate in Advanced English, and the Certificate of Proficiency in English. In each test, the interaction begins with a warm-up, in which the examinees introduce themselves to the interlocutor or, if they know each other, they introduce each other. This is followed by two pair interaction tasks. In the Cambridge First Certificate, the first is based on colour photographs and involves each examinee comparing and contrasting two of them while the other examinee listens and then makes a short comment. The second task uses one or more photographs, artwork or computer graphics as a basis for a pair interaction task where the examinees come to a jointly negotiated conclusion (UCLES, 2001a). The examinees spend three minutes on the first picture-based task and four minutes on the second. The final task in the test is a three-way discussion with the two examinees and the interlocutor about a general theme that is related to the earlier discussion.

Other pair tasks might be instructing another examinee to draw a graph or a route on a map, constructing a story together when each of the speakers knows half of it, or making a joint decision or recommendation on an issue presented in the task material. While contrived to some extent, these tasks generate peer-to-peer talk, and because the participants do not know the information the other one has they provide a genuine purpose for the interaction. In less structured task formats, the information to be discussed may not be given in the task materials. For example, pairs may be asked to discuss a topic from a number of angles for a certain amount of time. In most if not all types of pair tasks, the speaker roles and responsibilities are different from those of the interviewee, and this is how the tasks offer broader evidence about the examinees' interaction skills.

While paired tasks have many advantages, there are also challenges. The examinees' talk is almost inevitably influenced by the other participant's personality, communication style and possibly also language level. The concern is that all test takers may not get an equal opportunity to show their speaking skills at their best (Weir, 1993: 55–56; Iwashita, 1999: 53). When the effects of different pair characteristics on scores have been investigated, the results have shown that the influence is small, and sometimes different studies provide contradictory results about what characteristics boost or deflate them (e.g. Berry, 1997; Iwashita, 1999; O'Sullivan, 2002). This may be because there are so many variables that their combined effect on different individuals is difficult to predict, but also because raters probably take note of the different interaction features and they affect their ratings in complex ways. The upshot from all this for classroom testing is that scores from paired interactions must be interpreted with care, and if there is more than one test, different pairings could be tried at different times. For formal tests of speaking, it means that validity studies have to be conducted about the possible effect of differences between pairs on the scores. This is based on the rationale that, if the scores are interpreted as generalisable evidence about each examinee's ability to interact with peers, the scores should not be affected by different communication partners.

Another feature of paired tasks that testers often feel uncertain about is the amount of responsibility that they give to the examinees, who are not trained in interview techniques. But control over exactly what will be said in the interaction is not the issue with paired tasks. Rather, what the developers need to ensure is that the instructions and task materials are clear enough to facilitate the discussion and that the examinees know what kind of performances will earn them good results. In addition, the developers may want to make sure that they have a safety mechanism in place in case a pair task fails to work for some unpredictable reason. This could be an interlocutor asking additional questions if one of the examinees has said too little, or a spare task that can be used if a pair just cannot get started at all on the standard task. These solutions are only possible if there is an examiner monitoring the pair work, however. If the pair work is done in a language classroom without direct teacher monitoring and it proves later that the task has not worked with one pair, new testing, possibly with a different pair, might be the easiest solution.

On a fundamental level, the question about the effect of the interlocutor on an examinee's performance can be asked about examiner-led speaking tests as well. It may be unfair to rate the examinees only when the test discourse is jointly created (Brown, 2003; McNamara, 1997). The interviewer's proficiency level is often not an issue, but personality and communication style certainly are. Brown (2003) showed several examples of this in a conversation analytic study where one examinee was tested by two different interviewers. One was explicit and supportive. She made elaboration requests clearly (*Tell me more about...*) and indicated comprehension and interest in her feedback turns. This helped the examinee say more and thus made her appear a willing and able communication partner, which the raters recognised in their scores. The other interviewer's questioning strategies were much more inexplicit. He asked closed questions (*yes–no* and *or* questions) more frequently and he often asked for elaboration indirectly by repeating a phrase that the examinee had used. The examinee often (mis)interpreted this as a request for confirmation and simply said *yes* or *mm* instead of elaborating. The interviewer paused to give the examinee more time to respond, and this created an impression of a dysfluent and reticent speaker. The raters marked the performance accordingly. The upshot for examination boards is an encouragement to analyse interlocutor behaviour and give them feedback to ensure fair testing conditions for all examinees.

Like pair work, group interaction tasks are also generally well received by learners (e.g. Shohamy et al., 1986; Fulcher, 1996), but perhaps because of administrative concerns about managing the sizes of groups and the mixture of ability levels in them, they are not often used in formal tests of speaking (Reves, 1991). In classroom assessment, however, group discussions, or individual presentations followed by group discussion, can be quite practical, and they serve the purpose of practising speaking and generating learner talk quite well. They are also efficient, and they can support learning quite well, especially if learners also participate in the assessment process.

As an example, Fulcher (1996) used discussion on education in the participants' home countries as a group task. At the start of the task, each student received a task card with some ideas for the content of the discussion, and they were given 10 minutes to prepare individually what they were going to say. After the preparation time, they were invited to discuss the subject with each other for 15 minutes. Beyond being encouraged to listen to each other and ask questions, they were not given instructions about how to structure the discussion.

As is evident from the example above, once a group task is started, it is likely to go on for quite a long time, perhaps up to 30 minutes. Part of this may be spent in preparation, but the discussion is also going to take quite a while because all the participants must have a chance to talk for a sufficient length of time so their performance can be assessed. It is common that, once the task gets going, the examiner does not intervene in the discussion but, instead, the examinees manage the discussion themselves. Thus, as with pair tasks, it is important that the task is sufficiently clear and sufficiently motivating for all participants, and that everyone understands the rules for managing the interaction and providing each with other opportunities to speak. Moreover, if the participants also take part in the assessment, they need to know what criteria they should apply. One way of doing this is creating the criteria together with the examinees, or modifying a basic set of criteria that the teacher brings into the class. Responsibility for monitoring the progress of the testing may be an issue, and if several groups are working at the same time the discussions might be taped, or the groups might be asked to report back to the whole class. The tapes can serve in assessment, but they may also be used in self-reflection of speaking skills, for example by asking students to transcribe sections of their talk. Lynch (2001) found that this activity was engaging for the students and helpful for the development of their speaking skills.

Pedagogic tasks or real-life simulation?

When designing speaking tasks, it may be useful to distinguish between **'pedagogic'** or **'language-focused' tasks**, which are created specifically for certain types of language use, often to enable learning or assessment, and **'real-life'** or **'target' tasks**, which simulate language use outside the classroom (Nunan, 1989). For example, learner A is given a simple graph with a blue triangle, a red square and a black circle arranged diagonally across a page (or a ball, a hula hoop, a skipping rope and a water pistol at the four corners of a square, or whatever), and told to instruct learner B to draw the objects in the right configuration on an empty page, or learner B is given a drawing of a man's face and told to instruct learner A to draw it, possibly on a page that provides some of the basic lines such as the jaw line and the neck to help get the drawing started. The activity has an indirect relationship to real-life instruction-giving tasks, yet it is meaning-focused and communicative. It makes one of the learners instruct the other and both of them collaborate in checking that the instruction receiver is able to follow. If instruction-giving has been taught before the test, this may be a highly relevant activity to test. Topics can be varied by changing the picture or graph that the instruction-giver is talking from. To make the picture, the task designer can simply draw the figures, or cut pictures out of magazines and arrange them on a page.

'Real-life' or 'target' tasks replicate the essentials of non-test language use in the assessment situation. This is usually done through simulation or role-play. Typical real-life tasks in formal tests put examinees in their professional role while the examiners act as customers, patients, guests, or other likely people who might interact with the examinee in the test language in occupational contexts. The factory tour scenario in Chapter 1, for example, was a simulation – quite an elaborate one at that, as it was set up in a school workshop with an actual production line. The medical professionals' English test that Brown and Lumley (1997) investigated was a work-related role-play.

The development of real-life test tasks requires careful analysis of the target language-use situations and, as McNamara (1996) points out, a careful balancing between the linguist's view of necessary language ability and the professional's view of appropriate professional communication. He distinguishes between performance testing in the strong and weak sense, such that **strong performance testing** replicates the real-life language-use event and also employs real-world criteria for judging task success, whereas proof of having enough language ability would be enough to gain a good score in a **weak performance test**. In a simulation where a doctor should reassure a patient, being able to use appropriate language would suffice in a weak performance test, whereas the examiner in a strong performance test would have to judge whether he/she felt reassured in the situation. The decision about which criteria to use depends on the intended use of the test. The criteria in most language tests follow the weak performance testing logic, probably because both the testers and the examinees recognise that a language test is a language test. With formal tests the documentation should make clear which type of criteria are used, and in classroom assessment it would be helpful to discuss the differences between strong and weak performance criteria so that the learners understand how their performances are evaluated – in the test and outside it.

In learning-related assessment, simulations may also be undertaken in pairs or groups of four, as in the factory tour example in Chapter 1. Only a few tasks are suitable for this type of application, but when it is possible the advantage is an expanded role for the learners. Task design and discussions about relevant assessment criteria, practising for the test, the actual testing activity and the post-test reflection and evaluation blend together and serve the general goal of supporting the participants' learning.

Role-plays in testing can also be less elaborate, as when examinees are asked to play the role of a passenger on a train and interact with a fellow passenger, go to a restaurant and order a meal, or buy something in a shop. These tasks are aimed at finding out how the examinees can cope with certain common language-use tasks and situations. Role cards may be used to provide cues for the participants, and these may be quite elaborate if one of the examinees plays the role of a service provider, such as a waiter. If the examinees are ready to play-act in this sense, the task may generate some fairly genuine social interaction, but some artificiality is unavoidable because the speakers are playing a role for the purposes of the test. This should be taken into account in assessing the performances.

Construct-based or task-based assessment of speaking?

In teaching and testing, it is traditional to speak of the four skills of listening, reading, writing and speaking, and to practise and assess them separately. The simplification is intended to make learning and assessment more efficient by focusing on one type of skill at a time. In language use in general, however, all the skills are often used more or less at the same time, and even in teaching and testing learners may be asked to read or listen to something before they start to interact with each other. Nevertheless, testers may sometimes want to take care not to let the other skills influence the scores too much. This is important if they need to make sure that the scores really reflect skills in speaking or spoken inter- action, and not reading or listening as well. Even when this does not matter so much, the object of assessment in this approach to testing is language ability in a broad sense. Because of the primary focus on the construct of language ability, this is called the **construct-based approach** to assessment.

An alternative way of approaching assessment is to use tasks and language-use contexts as the first level of categorisation. Tests in this approach could be about conducting patient discussions during medical appointments, for example, which comprises part of a medical doctor's communication skills. This is called the **task-based approach** to assess- ment, and it is used especially in professional contexts (see e.g. Douglas, 2000). However, it can also be used in language classrooms in secondary and tertiary education (e.g. Norris *et al.*, 2002; Robinson, 2001), and it may underlie specific purpose tests such as the Canadian Academic English Language (CAEL) Assessment (CAEL, 2002). The scores in task- based language assessment speak about the examinees' ability to deal with the demands of the situations and tasks that are included in the test.

The difference between construct-based and task-based assessment is the position of tasks in designing assessments. Do they define what is tested, or are they the means of getting the examinees to talk so that their speaking skills can be assessed? The choice depends on the intended use of the scores. If they are used for judging the level of the examinees' speaking skills in general, the primary design principle should be the construct, but, as Bachman (2002) points out, tasks also need to inform the design of the assessment to make the description of the skills tested concrete enough. Strongly task-based assessment is useful when the target language-use situation is easy to define, as in the case of profes- sional qualification examinations or entrance tests for study or employ- ment, and also in teaching situations when teaching has been focused on a certain type of task and the teacher needs information about how well the students have learned the relevant skills (Norris, 2002). The two per- spectives should not be seen as conflicting, however. Ultimately, the test developers need to include both construct and task considerations in the design and development of speaking tests.

The decision about task-based or construct-based assessment affects the way the test developers talk about their test. Is it a test of speaking that focuses on narratives, or a test of telling a story? By the same token, the decision also affects the wording and conceptualisation of assessment criteria – I will discuss this in the next chapter. For formal tests, moreover, it affects the kind of validity evidence that needs to be gathered to support the score interpretations. With task-based tests, the developers need to show that the content of the test tasks is representative of the demands of the corresponding task outside the test situation, and that the scoring reflects this. Bachman (2002) warns that this may be very difficult, because tasks in most 'real-life' domains are so complex and diverse. If it is difficult to define what ought to be tested, it is also difficult to say how far the scores from the test can be generalised to the examinees' performance on the relevant real-life tasks. If the tasks are narrower and more closely defined, however, as can be the case with classroom tasks such as descriptions or presentations, the generalisation may be easier. With construct-based tests, the developers need to define the construct with reference to theoretical models, course syllabuses, and/or careful needs analysis, and then provide content-, construct- and process-related evidence that the language skills engaged in test performance and expressed in the test scores correspond to this definition. This is also challenging, but the basis for defining the construct is more secure because the reference frameworks of theories and course syllabuses already exist. While the emphasis on construct or task considerations may vary depending on the testing situation, the bottom line is that both considerations need to be included in test development.

Stand-alone or integrated assessment of speaking?

Many speaking tests clearly concentrate on spoken interaction or spoken production, and avoid mixing extended reading, writing or listening activities with the speaking tasks, as mentioned above. Other tests – typically task-based ones – *do* explicitly include tasks that are frequent in the target language-use situation and that involve combinations of reading, listening and/or writing activities with speaking. These are called **integrated** tasks, and the motivation for using them is typically the desire to make language use in the test authentic. If examinees do well on these tasks, they have shown that they possess the skills and abilities required in the situation. If they do not, it may not be clear whether it is their reading or speaking skills, for example, that failed them. However, the testers' intention may well be to evaluate their ability to deal with the simulated situation.

Brown *et al.* (2001) studied the differences between stand-alone and integrated speaking tasks on tape-based tests, and found that they gave rise to somewhat different perceptions of skills in raters. Integrated tasks made the raters attend to the examinees' comprehension of the input material and its effect on fluency and on quality and organisation of content. This seems highly appropriate given the nature of integrated tasks, even if, at the same time, it meant that the examinees did less well on the integrated than the stand-alone tasks, possibly because of the increased cognitive load. A more fundamental assessment problem was that there was far less agreement between the raters about final ratings. Brown *et al.* (2001) noted this as a reliability problem and suggested that it might be solved by more detailed, task-specific rating scales and/or rater training that would clarify exactly how the content of the input should be reflected in the performances.

Test mode: Live or tape-based?

The most common way of assessing speaking is in live, face-to-face interaction. As discussed above, this can be done in several configurations, including one-to-one interview, paired tasks between examinees and group testing. More rarely, live interaction can be tested through the telephone or through video teleconferencing. This is normally only done when it is difficult to bring the tester and the examinee face-to-face for geographical reasons, but sometimes telephone testing can be done on purpose, for example if it is important for a job to test how well the examinees can handle themselves over the phone.

The main characteristic of the live test mode is that interaction in it is two-directional. Each speaker's turn is a reaction to the previous turn, and if clarifications or other modifications are needed to the general interaction plan these can be made. The construct assessed is clearly related to spoken *interaction*. Tape-based testing, in contrast, is one-directional. The examinee is expected to accommodate to the tape but the tape cannot accommodate to the examinee. Thus, it only covers some aspects of interactive speaking and the construct is more clearly concerned with spoken *production*. Tape-based tests often include **monologic speaking tasks**, where one speaker produces a long turn alone without interacting with other speakers, but they also typically include extracts of situations where the examinees say something in a particular situation, possibly in response to another speaker whose turn is heard from the tape.

Tape-based testing is usually only used when there are large numbers of examinees so that it would be difficult to get enough live testers to interact with all of them. Developing a master tape for a tape-based test requires a large amount of work, but once it has been produced, the exact same test can be administered at any number of test locations at the same time, and also at different times, as long as test security is maintained, for example by drawing tasks from a large pool so that tests administered at different times are not exactly the same. The efficiency of administration and the comparability of the test across administrations are the most significant strengths of tape-based testing.

One question that researchers have asked about the two testing modes is how far they test the same skills. Studies into this have indicated that there is considerable overlap, at least in the sense that people who score high in one mode also score high in the other (see e.g. Stansfield and Kenyon, 1991; Wigglesworth and O'Loughlin, 1993). However, as discourse events and assessment experiences, the two modes differ (Shohamy, 1994; O'Loughlin, 2001). When the examinees talk to a tape recorder, their language is a little more literate and less oral-like, and many of them feel more anxious about the test because everything they say is recorded and the only channel they have for communicating is speaking – no gestures or expressions can be used. Nevertheless, many examinees also feel that a tape-based test can be a good test of their speaking skills, even if they prefer live testing.

In a practical sense, the sheer amount of work required for developing a tape-based test makes it unlikely for classroom testing. For formal tests, it is a possibility, especially if the practical circumstances make it difficult to arrange live tests. If a formal test is very important, it may be useful to include both modes in order to get the best of both worlds, the interactiveness and accommodation of the live interaction and the strict comparability of testing processes in the tape-based test.

The issue of task difficulty

'Difficulty' is an intuitively appealing concept to use when we think about people's ability to deal with tasks. Some tasks are more difficult than others in whatever area of life: juggling four balls is more difficult than juggling three, and doing so while standing on your head is more difficult than when standing upright, for example. But is riding a one-wheel bicycle more difficult than juggling four balls, and is performing circus acts more difficult than acting in plays? Difficulty is not a direct characteristic of tasks; rather, it is the sum of task characteristics and the conditions under which someone performs the task (standing on their head or on their two feet) in relation to the person's ability in the skills that it requires. Difficulty is nevertheless a concept that we use in designing teaching curricula and tests. We want syllabuses to proceed from easier tasks to more difficult ones to support learning, and we want parallel versions of a test to have equally difficult tasks to be fair to all examinees.

Because of this wish to do right by learners and test takers, some researchers have designed studies to find out how to manipulate the difficulty of speaking tasks. They have investigated features such as the complexity of task materials (Brown and Yule, 1983; Brown *et al.*, 1984), task familiarity, cognitive complexity and planning time (Foster and Skehan, 1996; Skehan and Foster, 1997; 2001; Wigglesworth, 1997; Elder *et al.*, 2002), task complexity (Robinson, 1995; Norris *et al.*, 2000), and interlocutor effects (Berry, 1997; Brown and Lumley, 1997). While some differences that influence scores have been found, the effects have been small, and the findings from different studies sometimes contradict each other. Task difficulty has proven difficult to predict, probably because of the complex way in which speaking scores are formed. As discussed in Chapter 1, they are based on two interactive processes: the first one between the examination participant(s), the interlocutor(s) and the task, and the second between the performance, the rater and the scoring criteria. All of these factors and interactions have an influence on the scores. Moreover, the differences between performing tasks in teaching and testing situations mean that the outcomes of studies of task difficulty in one area do not necessarily generalise into the other (Elder *et al.*, 2002).

Nevertheless, the studies on speaking-task difficulty have yielded some useful advice for the planning of speaking tasks, and possibly some general guidelines for manipulating task difficulty, as long as comparisons are made between tasks of the same type. In a series of studies, Brown and Yule (1983) found that the number of objects or individuals to be discussed affected task difficulty. It was easier to tell (and understand) a story about an accident that involved two or three cars than one involving four or five. However, what was also significant was the distinguishability of the objects or individuals. If a story was about a boy and a girl, it was easier to tell than one about two girls, which again was easier than a story about three girls (simply because the students had to use more words to make it clear who did what). The number and complexity of events also affected difficulty, and in description tasks simplicity and symmetry of spatial structures was important. In sum, the more elements, factors or events there are in the task material, the more complex the language that the speakers need to use, and therefore the more challenging the task. Thus, if there are several picture-based narrative tasks that are intended to be parallel, the developers should check that each picture sequence involves a similar number of characters and events to make the tasks more comparable.

Moreover, when investigating storytelling, Brown and colleagues found that causal links between elements, e.g. a plot in a sequence of events, makes an account more meaningful and easier to tell and understand. Interestingly, the presence of a plot also made the language of the speakers more complex (Brown, 1989). One of the tasks that was used in studying this was a three-scene video-based story about delivering letters in an office. The students who were not given a hint to look for a plot in the events saw three women, two of whom delivered letters. One of them also opened a letter and took some money out of it. The accounts that the students gave of the events were plain and short. The speakers did not give many details to distinguish the women from each other. In contrast, the students who were told that they were going to see a story about someone stealing something gave much more detailed accounts and clearly distinguished between 'the thief' and the others. They saw the thief's actions as intentional, and they made a point of this in their stories. Consequently, they talked more about the events, and the language they used was more complex than that used by the first group. Thus, if there is a plot in speaking test materials, it might make sense to lead the examinees on to it in the instructions, to make the task work the same way for all of them.

Overview of speaking task types

Initial task design becomes concrete when the designers turn their attention to task types. Since this is an important part of test design, I will give a brief summary of speaking task types in this chapter. Chapter 7 will provide concrete examples of the types and discuss task development. I will discuss the task types under two headings, open-ended and structured tasks. The distinction builds on the relative amount of structure that the tasks provide for the test discourse. **Open-ended speaking tasks** guide the discussion but allow room for different ways of fulfilling the task requirements. They typically call for a stretch of talk, which can be either a number of turns between speakers or a single long speaking turn. **Structured speaking tasks**, in contrast, specify quite precisely what the examinees should say. They typically call for limited production, and often it is possible to give an exhaustive list of acceptable responses.

Open-ended speaking tasks

The main purpose in open-ended tasks is to get the examinees to *do* something with language as an indication of their skills. This can be a relatively long activity, such as giving a presentation, or a short, function-based action like making a request. The longer the activity, the more potential freedom the examinees have for responding to it, though task instructions may provide some content guidelines for them.

One way of dividing open-ended speaking tasks into task types is discourse types, as discussed earlier in this chapter. *Description, narrative, instruction, comparison, explanation, justification, prediction,* and *decision* tasks can have pictures or written material as their basis, or an examiner may name a topic for the examinee. The Oral Proficiency Interview (Proficiency Standards Division, 1999), for example, includes a description task, and the interviewers are instructed to ask the examinees to describe something that is familiar to them, such as their aunt's house if the examinee has mentioned an aunt earlier, or a favourite nephew. The interviewers do not know whether the description is factually accurate, but this is the case in most 'real-world' situations when somebody is asked to describe something. The criterion is rather whether they can picture what the examinee is describing. When the material is provided by a picture, the content of the examinee's talk must also correspond to the testers' expectations.

All the tasks listed above can be completed between an interviewer and an examinee or between two examinees. If they are given to two examinees, it might be useful to create an information gap between them by providing each of them with part of the content only. Decision tasks, such as recommending a course of action to someone who has written to an advice column in a magazine, could also conceivably be done in a group of three or four people. With a little bit of planning time, any of the tasks could also be included in a tape-based test of speaking. The talk created in this context would be different, because it is clearly a monologue with no immediate listeners to interact with, but some of the language activities would be the same in all contexts.

Another category of open-ended tasks is *role-play*. As discussed above, some of these tasks may simulate the professional context of the examinees and put the testers in the role of their clients or non-expert acquaintances. Other role-play tasks simulate social or service situations such as buying something or going to a restaurant, which have a fairly predictable structure. These may need an elaborate script, at least if one of the examinees has the role of a service provider. From the point of view of clients, the situations are fairly predictable, and this is why they are sometimes used even in tape-mediated tests in the form of simulated discussions. The examinees hear the service provider's turns from the tape and respond according to the standard expectations. The intention in role-play tasks is to simulate reality. In professional contexts, the aim is to assess how well the examinees can cope with the language demands of their profession. In social role-plays, the task design usually includes some social twist so that the examinees' ability to deal with social complications or unpredictable turns of events can be assessed. A task that combines some elements of role-play and the previous category of discourse-type tasks is giving a presentation (professional) or making a speech, such as speaking to someone on their birthday (social). The examinee assumes a role and speaks at some length, structuring their talk according to the conventions of the talk type and using the social conventions required by the role-play situation.

A semi-structured task that focuses on socially or functionally complex language use is **reacting in situations**. The examinees read or hear the social situation where they should imagine themselves to be, and they are asked to say what they would say in the situation. The responses require the use of formulaic language but also the ability to modify expressions, as the situations often include a social twist. For example, the examinees might be asked to complain about the noisiness of a neighbour's party while they have to study, knowing that they will themselves be having a party at home the following week. This task type is used in tape-mediated and face-to-face tests, but because there are usually a handful of different situations, they fit tape-based tests better, as it is difficult for the face-to-face tester to change roles credibly too many times.

Structured speaking tasks

Structured speaking tasks are the speaking equivalent of multiple choice tasks. The expected answers are usually short, and the items tend to focus on one narrow aspect of speaking at a time. While these tasks cannot assess the unpredictable and creative elements of speaking, their strength is comparability, as they are exactly the same for all examinees, and with the help of a scoring key they can be scored fairly with very little training.

In the most highly structured speaking tasks, the examinees get everything that they should say from the task materials. Since the testers know what they are going to say, their responses can be justifiably judged against this norm. **Reading aloud** usually focuses on pronunciation, and while comprehensibility may be an important criterion, norms and expectations about rhythm, stress, intonation and accuracy of individual sounds usually have an influence in the background. Another structured task, **sentence repetition**, is more processing-oriented. There is no written input, but rather the examinees hear a sentence and repeat it immediately afterwards. A task is usually composed of a series of sentences, which become longer and more complex as the task progresses. To do well, the learners need to understand each sentence and divide it into a small number of meaningful chunks that they can remember and repeat accurately. Because of the emphasis on processing and memory, sentence repetition is more typically used in psychological tests, processing studies and neurolinguistic research than in language tests. However, it is one of the tasks in Phone Pass (see www.ordinate.com), a telephone-mediated test that is scored automatically by a speech processing databank. To create a sentence-repetition task that provides interpretable scores, the developers need to know how to make the items more complex in a principled way, most likely following a theory of speech processing.

Tasks that give a little more freedom for the examinees to decide what to say include **sentence completion** and **factual short-answer questions**. The focus in sentence completion is on grammatical knowledge and contextual understanding, as the examinee response has to complete the sentence in a way that makes sense. Short answers focus a little less on grammatical knowledge, though the response has to be a self-standing utterance, and more on understanding the context and providing the required information. **Reacting to phrases** focuses on knowledge of phrases and social acceptability. These tasks typically include common question–answer or comment–response sequences such as greetings or apology–acceptance routines, technically known as adjacency pairs. The test provides the first turn, and the examinees are expected to provide the response that completes the routine in a socially acceptable way.

Structured speaking tasks are commonly found in tape-based tests and much more rarely used in face-to-face testing. In addition to the tasks listed above, a tape-based test would also typically contain some less structured tasks such as reacting in situations and giving a presentation or talking about a topic. These give the testers a longer stretch of the examinees' speech and thus evidence about their ability to keep going and express their thoughts independently.

Task-related documents and materials

The initial task design provides the general action plan for developing a speaking assessment, but before it can be put into practice a number of materials need to be created to direct the activities of the examinees and examiners. These include:

- the rubric and the instructions to examinees;
- the task materials, which the examinees use while performing the tasks (if relevant);
- an interaction outline, which gives guidelines or scripts for examiners about the content and wording of questions or prompts;
- plans and instructions for administration.

Test rubric and instructions to participants

The **test rubric** defines the structure of an assessment and provides instructions to participants about what they should do (Bachman and Palmer, 1996: 50). As they say:

> The test rubric includes those characteristics of the test that provide the structure for particular test tasks and that indicate how test takers are to proceed in accomplishing the tasks. In a test task these need to be made as explicit and clear as possible, while in language use these characteristics are generally implicit. For this reason, rubric may be a characteristic for which there is relatively little correspondence

between language use tasks and test tasks. The characteristics of rubric include:

1 the structure of the test, that is, how the test itself is organized,
2 instructions,
3 the duration of the test as a whole and the individual tasks, and
4 how the language that is used will be evaluated, or scored.

The rubric is a tool for the assessment designers, and the part of it that is visible for test participants is instructions and any other test information material that the developers may produce.

When writing instructions, the assessment designers need to consider how much about each of the rubric features has to be explained to the participants. On the one hand, instructions need to be brief and clear. On the other, it is fairer to the participants if they know at least something about all of these elements so that they do not need to guess what the assessment is about. In learning-related contexts, some of the information can be provided before the actual assessment situation, possibly even created or agreed together with the learners, whereas in formal tests the developers provide all the information. The instructions in particular are important for task development because they set the scene for how the participants will perceive the task and their own performance on it.

Here is an example of general instructions for a classroom speaking test.

SPOKEN INTERACTION TEST IN ENGLISH*

The test will be held in room 14. It is important to turn up for your test session punctually.

The test is given to two pupils at a time, because most of it involves paired interaction. It is composed of the following parts: a short warm-up discussion, talking about a picture or a news article, and a paired discussion (role-play).

The test is not impossibly challenging and no one needs to feel tense about it. When you are talking, do not worry about occasional mistakes, and if ever you can't find the most appropriate word, just work around the problem by saying it in a different way. It is important to speak as much as you can; your comprehensibility and level of fluency are the most important factors in the assessment.

There is a short preparation time, which is intended to allow you to familiarise yourself with the test tasks. It is important to be there on time for the start of your preparation time.

* instructions translated from Finnish original

These instructions are fairly concise because the teacher and students have talked about the test and test preparation in class. With formal tests, information about how to prepare for the test and how to do well on it may be more elaborate (see e.g. *Test takers' Preparation Guide* (CAEL, 2000) at www.carleton.ca/slals/cael.htm).

In addition to general instructions, the developers need to devise task instructions. These can be written if the task material is presented on paper, or the examiner can give them orally. They direct the examinees to the specifics of a task. As an example, the task instructions for the picture description task in the above test look like this.

Talking about a picture
Describe the picture to your partner in as much detail as possible. Then talk about your own impression of the picture (what the people are thinking, what has happened before the picture was taken, what will happen next, etc.).

Then show the picture to your partner and ask him/her to comment on both your description and the picture itself.

Task materials

By **task materials**, I refer to any written or picture-based materials that are given to the examinees during a speaking assessment to provide contents, outlines or starting points for the test discourse. These include role-play cards, menus, schedules, suggested topics or sub-topics for a discussion, short written texts, pictures and picture sequences, or whatever materials that the examiners provide to the examinees to generate talk.

Task materials are important because they provide a way for the test designers to guide the talk during the test. For the same reason, they are also time-consuming to develop, because they need to be inspiring enough to generate talk in the first place, structured enough so they really generate the talk that the developers intend, and unpredictable enough so the examinees cannot rehearse their performance on these particular topics and tasks.

With picture-based tasks, the developers can work with existing pictures or draw new ones. Matching testing needs with existing pictures is not easy, however, and teachers who have used them report that for several months before their intended test they keep their eyes open for possible pictures whenever they read anything. Cartoons, which may appear a good choice at first, can pose problems because they often play on visual concepts or a combination of visuals and speech bubbles to tell an amusing story. To reach the same level of amusement in a re-telling of the cartoon on the test requires verbal creativity beyond general speaking skills, and if speech bubbles are included the examinees need to be deft with reported speech. It may also be that a good cartoon story is told in a couple of sentences when it is given orally. In educational settings where the examinees do not pay for the testing, copyright is not really an issue. With published tests, however, it is, and this is one reason why pictures in them are most often specially created for the test. This can indeed be a viable alternative to using ready-made pictures, as it enables the test developers to design all the contents of the picture. The actual drawing, painting or photography calls for artistic creativity, of course, and the test developers do not always have it. Testing boards usually hire artists, while in educational settings the art teacher may be able to help.

Whether the developers use existing or newly created pictures, trialling the task before actual use in the test is a very good idea. Different people can have surprisingly different interpretations of a picture and different strategies for telling a story related to a picture sequence. After trialling, the task instructions or examiner prompts may need to be modified. Trialling is also useful with text-based task materials. These tend to be less work-intensive to create, but they have their own challenges. Design considerations here include the language in which the material is given, the level of formality and lexical demand of the text, and the amount of text that the examinees are required to read. I will give examples of both types of task materials in Chapter 7.

Interaction outline

Whenever there is an examiner involved in an oral test, either as an interviewer or as a facilitator to get the test interaction started, the test developers need to write instructions for them regarding what to do and say. These often take the form of an outline for the test, possibly with some suggested prompts. The outline (which is sometimes called an 'interlocutor frame' because it guides the interlocutor's talk in the test) is important because in a test situation the examiner's role is to structure the discourse and, to be fair to all examinees, the structure should be similar in all of them. Here is an example of an interaction outline from the classroom test discussed above.

Time	Phase and prompts
2–3 min	**Warm-up**
	Greeting and seating
	How are you doing? How has your day been today?
	What are you planning to do during the rest of the day? (+ follow-up)
	Explain interview structure: description/narration task, discussion, role play
4–5 min	**Description/narration**
	Have you read the instructions for this task? Any questions?
	Please start.
2–3 min	**Discussion**
	(Nothing if they start themselves; otherwise: Please go on to discussing the themes that you took up in your talk just now.
	(Support with questions if the pair cannot get the discussion started, e.g. So, do you think about X sometimes? / How do you feel about X? / Does X have relevance in our life here at school, do you think?)
	(If one dominates, ask the other a question or two at the end.)
	Thank you __ and __; now let's go on to the role-play.
4–5 min	**Role-play**
	(Nothing unless one or both are completely stuck)
1 min	**Closing**
	Have either of you thought about something like this as a possible thing to do? / Has something like this happened to either of you or anyone you know?
	(If yes, how realistic / what happened?; if not, why not?)
	Do you have any plans for the summer?
	Thank you, goodbye

This outline is fairly sparse, because the two pair tasks constitute most of the test discourse and the examinees read instructions and guidelines for these. Moreover, there is only one tester, so comparability between interlocutors is not an issue; the teacher just needs to be consistent in her questions.

In large-scale formal tests, interlocutor skills and comparability between different examiners are central fairness concerns. The test structure is usually carefully designed, and interlocutors are trained in questioning techniques and examined and certified before they can begin to act as testers for the system. Initial training periods of a few days are common, and in one case – the Oral Proficiency Interview as practised at the Defense Language Institute – the initial training lasts twelve days. Following this training, the interviewers are expected to have internalised the interaction outline so that they do not need a written version of it to glance at while they test. In other tests, the interlocutors can have the outline handy during the test, although they are normally advised not to make too much use of it or especially read directly from it. This is because while the test is structured, the interaction should also be genuinely interactive, and that is only possible if both speakers attend to each other's speech as a priority.

Preparing an interaction outline makes the test developers plan the talk during the test in considerable detail. This offers a good opportunity for them to check that the test will really yield the kind of sample of language use that their initial design calls for. If it is possible to conduct a trial interview or two, the usability of the interaction outline can be tested before actual use. Thus, actual test takers do not need to act as guinea pigs while the interlocutor learns to use the outline.

Resources and procedures for administration

The way a speaking assessment is administered influences the examinees' experience of the test, and therefore it also has a bearing on what is tested. In the interests of fairness and comparability, the procedures should be planned beforehand. The goal is to ensure that all the participants, examinees and examiners included, know what they should do and when.

Big testing agencies often provide written instructions about administration, and the support personnel may be trained for their job. In classroom tests, the teacher is usually responsible for all the arrangements, and if the examinees need preparation time before the testing begins it is especially relevant to plan how the teacher can do this while also conducting the tests. In formal tests, the standardisation of conditions is important, and the administration procedures are likely to be monitored as part of the quality control procedures for the test.

The resources that need to be available when the assessment is arranged include:

- rooms (e.g. interview rooms, waiting rooms, language laboratory);
- equipment (tape recorders, video recorders, role-play props);

- personnel (e.g. interlocutors, administrators/assistants, technical assistance);
- time (i.e. how long the various people and material resources need to be available).

Making sure in good time that all the necessary resources are available helps the actual assessment situation flow smoothly. Because speaking tests are often administered to individuals or small groups, time management is particularly important, and this is supported by a testing schedule with interlocutor and examinee names and test times.

Summary

In this chapter, I have discussed the initial design of speaking tasks and outlined the documents and materials that assessment developers need before they can put them into practice. Task design is important because it makes the construct assessed in the test more tangible and because, for the examinees, tasks provide the context for the talk and guidelines about what they must *do* with language. I discussed types of talk and communicative functions as ways of describing and categorising speaking tasks, and then reviewed different ways of applying them to concrete tasks, including individual, pair and group tasks, and pedagogical and real-life tasks. Assessment developers will choose different designs according to the type of information they need, possibly guided by the tasks that the examinees know. The same rule, the type of information needed, should also decide whether construct-based or task-based assessment should be used. My conclusion regarding tape-based and live testing of speaking was that both have their advantages, though the heavy development demands of tape-based tests are only rewarded if the test has to be standardised and used by large numbers of examinees in many different locations. The discussion of task difficulty indicated that it is not a direct property of tasks but rather an outcome of two interactive processes, testing and rating. The first involves interactions between a large number of task features, the ability of the examinee, the performance of the interlocutor(s), and the conditions under which the tasks are performed. The second interaction involves all the properties of the test discourse, the contents of the scoring criteria, and the performance of the raters in interpreting these and applying them to the performances.

This chapter's discussion of tasks and task development covered the first half of the factors that influence the meaning of speaking scores. The second half consists of the scoring criteria and procedures. This is the topic of the next chapter.

CHAPTER FOUR

Speaking scales

Speaking scores express *how well* the examinees can speak the language being tested. They usually take the form of numbers, but they may also be verbal categories such as 'excellent' or 'fair'. In addition to the plain score, there is usually a shorter or longer statement that describes what each score means, and the series of statements from lowest to highest constitutes a **rating scale**. In this chapter, I will discuss the nature and development of rating scales for assessing speaking.

Since speaking scales are composed of an ascending series of levels, they are in some sense related to second language acquisition (SLA). However, they are not a direct application of SLA research, because the objective in SLA studies has not been to construct rating scales and the results are not clear enough to describe levels of acquisition in detail. In fact, given the complexity of language ability in general and speaking as part of it, it is not even certain how far it is possible to find clear learning paths that most or all learners can follow. North (1996) describes the challenge of developing rating scales as 'trying to describe complex phenomena in a small number of words on the basis of incomplete theory'. Furthermore, as Brindley (1998: 116) notes, it is not always easy to tell what scale descriptors are meant to describe – what learners *ought* to be able to do at each of the scale levels or what they *do* do. Thus, they may also reflect the developers' beliefs and assumptions about language learning. Nevertheless, since scales express the developers' understanding of how good performances differ from weak ones, they form part of their definition of the construct assessed in the test.

I will begin this chapter with some examples of speaking scales. Next, I will discuss methods of scale development. Finally, I will summarise some studies in SLA and language testing that can support the development of scales for assessing speaking.

Examples of speaking scales

The examples in this section are just that, examples. They are not given as ideal models, and should not be taken as such. Rather, they illustrate existing practice, at least in terms of scales that have been published. In discussing the examples, I will describe the practical purpose for which each was developed, and summarise the criticisms and defending arguments for them. I will also explain some scale-related terminology.

Scales are difficult to write both because of the scarcity of solid evidence about language learning and because of the need to summarise descriptors into short statements to make them easy to use. Thus, few rating scales used by examination boards are actually published. Rather, the boards publish the scale that they use for reporting the scores to the examinees, often together with a list of the features that are taken into account when rating. The boards may feel vulnerable because of potential weaknesses in their scale, or they may think that the language used in the rater-oriented scale is not suitable for the general public. It is legitimate for scales to differ depending on their main purpose and their target audience, and in fact it is useful to make different versions for different audiences rather than making one version suit all purposes (Alderson, 1991; North, 1996). Rater-oriented scales must help raters make consistent decisions; examinee-oriented scales give information about overall level and, possibly, particular strengths and weaknesses, while administrator-oriented scales give overall information in a concise form. Differences between versions include the terminology used, the amount of detail, and the focus in terms of *what* the examinees can do and *how well* they can do it (Council of Europe, 2001). The examples below illustrate this variation.

The National Certificate scale

The Finnish National Certificate scale (National Board of Education, 2002) is a holistic scale with six levels. **Holistic scales** express an overall

Table 4.1 *The National Certificate descriptive scale (National Board of Education, 2002)*

6	Speaks fluently with few if any non-native features, such as a foreign accent. Is capable of expressing even subtle nuances of meaning with precision, and also makes varied and appropriate use of idiomatic expressions. Is able to describe even a complicated topic and to include sub-themes in the description, to develop different viewpoints and to bring the presentation to an appropriate conclusion.
5	Speaks fluently without frequent obvious need to search for an expression. Delivery characterised by naturalness, coherence and appropriate length. Is able to present a clear and detailed description of even a complex topic. Can use idiomatic expressions and everyday expressions, and is able to express nuances fairly well.
4	Copes fairly well even in less familiar speech situations. Makes a distinction between formal and informal registers, at least to some extent. Is able to present and justify an opinion comprehensibly. Is able to talk about and describe sights, sounds and experiences. Is obliged only rarely to use circumlocutions in everyday communication because of inadequate language proficiency.
3	Copes with the most familiar speech situations and is able to take the initiative in everyday language-use situations. Speech may be quite slow but there are few unnatural pauses. Is comprehensible despite transferring native or foreign language structures and vocabulary to the target language. Pronunciation may clearly deviate from target language standards.
2	Copes with routine speaking situations that require a simple exchange of information. Nevertheless, the speaker's language proficiency considerably restricts the range of matters that can be dealt with. Successful communication of a message presupposes that the interlocutor is willing to help the speaker in forming the message. Pronunciation may deviate clearly from the target language norm, thus requiring special effort from the interlocutor and impeding successful communication.
1	Is able to ask and reply to simple questions dealing with immediate everyday needs. Can make use of simple polite forms. Copes with the very simplest speaking tasks, but communication is slow and very fragmented. Often obliged to resort to nonverbal means in order to be understood.

impression of an examinee's ability in one score. When holistic scales are used as rating scales, the raters may be asked to note several different features in the performances or pay attention to overall impression only. The scale in Table 4.1 is actually a descriptive scale intended for examinees and teaching professionals. It informs them about the rating scale used in the test without too much technical terminology. The actual rating scales for the test have not been published.

The National Certificate scale spans the whole ability range from early beginner to very advanced. However, these levels are not all covered in one test. Rather, there are three tests, each spanning two levels. One purpose of the scale is to inform potential examinees about the target levels so that they can choose an appropriate test for themselves.

Holistic scales are practical for decision-making because they only give one score. From a rater's perspective, holistic rating scales make rating quick because there is less to read and remember than in a complex grid with many criteria. Holistic scales are also flexible in that they allow many different combinations of strengths and weaknesses within a level. However, the other side of the coin is that they are not practical for diagnosing strengths and weaknesses in individual learners' performances. Moreover, there is a danger that the differences between levels may be what North (1996) calls 'word-processed'. That is, they may depend too much on quantifiers like *many*, *a few* and *few* or quality words like *adequately* and *well* and not enough on concrete differences. During scale development, critical comments and trials with using the scale are essential. I will discuss methods of scale development later in this chapter.

The ACTFL Speaking scale

The American Council for the Teaching of Foreign Languages (ACTFL) Speaking scale (ACTFL, 1999) is also a holistic scale, but here the same scale is used by raters and score users. It is used in foreign language programs in North American academia, particularly in colleges and universities. The scale has ten levels, which focus on the beginning and intermediate stages of language learning. There are four levels in the scale: Superior, Advanced, Intermediate and Novice. The three lower levels are divided into three sub-levels each. The aim is to show progress at the levels where most foreign language learners in the US educational contexts are.

The level descriptors mention the situations that the learners can cope with and the language activities they can do. They also describe the strong and weak points of their language. The strategy is copied from the Interagency Language Roundtable (ILR) scale (Clark and Clifford, 1988), the parent of this and most other speaking proficiency scales today. In a sense, the level descriptions define the outline of the ACTFL interview, because the testers need evidence about the skills mentioned at each of

Table 4.2 *ACTFL Proficiency Guidelines – Speaking (ACTFL, 1999)*

SUPERIOR
Speakers at the Superior level are able to communicate in the language with accuracy
and fluency in order to participate fully and effectively in conversations on a variety
of topics in formal and informal settings from both concrete and abstract
perspectives. They discuss their interests and special fields of competence, explain
complex matters in detail, and provide lengthy and coherent narrations, all with ease,
fluency, and accuracy. They explain their opinions on a number of topics of
importance to them, such as social and political issues, and provide structured
argument to support their opinions. They are able to construct and develop
hypotheses to explore alternative possibilities. When appropriate, they use extended
discourse without unnaturally lengthy hesitation to make their point, even when
engaged in abstract elaborations. Such discourse, while coherent, may still be
influenced by the Superior speakers' own language patterns, rather than those of the
target language. Superior speakers command a variety of interactive and discourse
strategies, such as turn-taking and separating main ideas from supporting
information through the use of syntactic and lexical devices, as well as intonational
features such as pitch, stress and tone. They demonstrate virtually no pattern of error
in the use of basic structures. However, they may make sporadic errors, particularly in
low-frequency structures and in some complex high-frequency structures more
common to formal speech and writing. Such errors, if they do occur, do not distract
the native interlocutor or interfere with communication.

ADVANCED HIGH
Speakers at the Advanced-High level perform all Advanced-level tasks with linguistic
ease, confidence and competence. They are able to consistently explain in detail and
narrate fully and accurately in all time frames. In addition, Advanced-High speakers
handle the tasks pertaining to the Superior level but cannot sustain performance at
that level across a variety of topics. They can provide a structured argument to
support their opinions, and they may construct hypotheses, but patterns of error
appear. They can discuss some topics abstractly, especially those relating to their
particular interests and special fields of expertise, but in general, they are more
comfortable discussing a variety of topics concretely. Advanced-High speakers may
demonstrate a well-developed ability to compensate for an imperfect grasp of some
forms or for limitations in vocabulary by the confident use of communicative
strategies, such as paraphrasing, circumlocution, and illustration. They use precise
vocabulary and intonation to express meaning and often show great fluency and ease
of speech. However, when they are called on to perform the complex tasks associated
with the Superior level over a variety of topics, their language, at times, breaks down
or proves inadequate, or they may avoid the task altogether, for example, by resorting
to simplification through the use of description or narration in place of argument or
hypothesis.

ADVANCED MID
Speakers at the Advanced-Mid level are able to handle with ease and confidence a
large number of communicative tasks. They participate actively in most informal and

Table 4.2 (*cont.*)

some formal exchanges on a variety of concrete topics relating to work, school, home, and leisure activities, as well as to events of current, public, and personal interest or individual relevance. Advanced-Mid speakers demonstrate the ability to narrate and describe in all major time frames (past, present, and future) by providing a full account, with good control of aspect, as they adapt flexibly to the demands of the conversation. Narration and description tend to be combined and interwoven to relate relevant and supporting facts in connected, paragraph-length discourse. Advanced-Mid speakers can handle successfully and with relative ease the linguistic challenges presented by a complication or unexpected turn of events that occurs within the context of a routine situation or communicative task with which they are otherwise familiar. Communicative strategies such as circumlocution or rephrasing are often employed for this purpose. The speech of Advanced-Mid speakers performing Advanced-level tasks is marked by substantial flow. Their vocabulary is fairly extensive although primarily generic in nature, except in the case of a particular area of specialization or interest. Dominant language discourse structures tend to recede, although discourse may still reflect the oral paragraph structure of their own language rather than that of the target language. Advanced-Mid speakers contribute to conversations on a variety of familiar topics, dealt with concretely, with much accuracy, clarity and precision, and they convey their intended message without misrepresentation or confusion. They are readily understood by native speakers unaccustomed to dealing with non-natives. When called on to perform functions or handle topics associated with the Superior level, the quality and/or quantity of their speech will generally decline. Advanced-Mid speakers are often able to state an opinion or cite conditions; however, they lack the ability to consistently provide a structured argument in extended discourse. Advanced-Mid speakers may use a number of delaying strategies, resort to narration, description, explanation or anecdote, or simply attempt to avoid the linguistic demands of Superior-level tasks.

ADVANCED LOW
Speakers at the Advanced-Low level are able to handle a variety of communicative tasks, although somewhat haltingly at times. They participate actively in most informal and a limited number of formal conversations on activities related to school, home, and leisure activities and, to a lesser degree, those related to events of work, current, public, and personal interest or individual relevance. Advanced-Low speakers demonstrate the ability to narrate and describe in all major time frames (past, present and future) in paragraph length discourse, but control of aspect may be lacking at times. They can handle appropriately the linguistic challenges presented by a complication or unexpected turn of events that occurs within the context of a routine situation or communicative task with which they are otherwise familiar, though at times their discourse may be minimal for the level and strained. Communicative strategies such as rephrasing and circumlocution may be employed in such instances. In their narrations and descriptions, they combine and link sentences into connected discourse of paragraph length. When pressed for a fuller account, they tend to grope and rely on minimal discourse. Their utterances are typically not longer than a single paragraph. Structure of the dominant language is

Table 4.2 (*cont.*)

still evident in the use of false cognates, literal translations, or the oral paragraph structure of the speakers' own language rather than that of the target language. While the language of Advanced-Low speakers may be marked by substantial, albeit irregular flow, it is typically somewhat strained and tentative, with noticeable self-correction and a certain grammatical roughness. The vocabulary of Advanced-Low speakers is primarily generic in nature. Advanced-Low speakers contribute to the conversation with sufficient accuracy, clarity, and precision to convey their intended message without misrepresentation or confusion, and it can be understood by native speakers unaccustomed to dealing with non-natives, even though this may be achieved through repetition and restatement. When attempting to perform functions or handle topics associated with the Superior level, the linguistic quality and quantity of their speech will deteriorate significantly.

INTERMEDIATE HIGH
Intermediate-High speakers are able to converse with ease and confidence when dealing with most routine tasks and social situations of the Intermediate level. They are able to handle successfully many uncomplicated tasks and social situations requiring an exchange of basic information related to work, school, recreation, particular interests and areas of competence, though hesitation and errors may be evident. Intermediate-High speakers handle the tasks pertaining to the Advanced level, but they are unable to sustain performance at that level over a variety of topics. With some consistency, speakers at the Intermediate-High level narrate and describe in major time frames using connected discourse of paragraph length. However, their performance of these Advanced-level tasks will exhibit one or more features of breakdown, such as the failure to maintain the narration or description semantically or syntactically in the appropriate major time frame, the disintegration of connected discourse, the misuse of cohesive devices, a reduction in breadth and appropriateness of vocabulary, the failure to successfully circumlocute, or a significant amount of hesitation. Intermediate-High speakers can generally be understood by native speakers unaccustomed to dealing with non-natives, although the dominant language is still evident (e.g. use of code-switching, false cognates, literal translations, etc.), and gaps in communication may occur.

INTERMEDIATE MID
Speakers at the Intermediate-Mid level are able to handle successfully a variety of uncomplicated communicative tasks in straightforward social situations. Conversation is generally limited to those predictable and concrete exchanges necessary for survival in the target culture; these include personal information covering self, family, home, daily activities, interests and personal preferences, as well as physical and social needs, such as food, shopping, travel and lodging. Intermediate-Mid speakers tend to function reactively, for example, by responding to direct questions or requests for information. However, they are capable of asking a variety of questions when necessary to obtain simple information to satisfy basic needs, such as directions, prices and services. When called on to perform functions or handle topics at the Advanced level, they provide some information but have

Table 4.2 (*cont.*)

difficulty linking ideas, manipulating time and aspect, and using communicative strategies, such as circumlocution. Intermediate-Mid speakers are able to express personal meaning by creating with the language, in part by combining and recombining known elements and conversational input to make utterances of sentence length and some strings of sentences. Their speech may contain pauses, reformulations and self-corrections as they search for adequate vocabulary and appropriate language forms to express themselves. Because of inaccuracies in their vocabulary and/or pronunciation and/or grammar and/or syntax, misunderstandings can occur, but Intermediate-Mid speakers are generally understood by sympathetic interlocutors accustomed to dealing with non-natives.

INTERMEDIATE LOW
Speakers at the Intermediate-Low level are able to handle successfully a limited number of uncomplicated communicative tasks by creating with the language in straightforward social situations. Conversation is restricted to some of the concrete exchanges and predictable topics necessary for survival in the target language culture. These topics relate to basic personal information covering, for example, self and family, some daily activities and personal preferences, as well as to some immediate needs, such as ordering food and making simple purchases. At the Intermediate-Low level, speakers are primarily reactive and struggle to answer direct questions or requests for information, but they are also able to ask a few appropriate questions. Intermediate-Low speakers express personal meaning by combining and recombining into short statements what they know and what they hear from their interlocutors. Their utterances are often filled with hesitancy and inaccuracies as they search for appropriate linguistic forms and vocabulary while attempting to give form to the message. Their speech is characterized by frequent pauses, ineffective reformulations and self-corrections. Their pronunciation, vocabulary and syntax are strongly influenced by their first language but, in spite of frequent misunderstandings that require repetition or rephrasing, Intermediate-Low speakers can generally be understood by sympathetic interlocutors, particularly by those accustomed to dealing with non-natives.

NOVICE HIGH
Speakers at the Novice-High level are able to handle a variety of tasks pertaining to the Intermediate level, but are unable to sustain performance at that level. They are able to manage successfully a number of uncomplicated communicative tasks in straightforward social situations. Conversation is restricted to a few of the predictable topics necessary for survival in the target language culture, such as basic personal information, basic objects and a limited number of activities, preferences and immediate needs. Novice-High speakers respond to simple, direct questions or requests for information; they are able to ask only a very few formulaic questions when asked to do so. Novice-High speakers are able to express personal meaning by relying heavily on learned phrases or recombinations of these and what they hear from their interlocutor. Their utterances, which consist mostly of short and sometimes incomplete sentences in the present, may be hesitant or inaccurate. On

Table 4.2 (*cont.*)

the other hand, since these utterances are frequently only expansions of learned material and stock phrases, they may sometimes appear surprisingly fluent and accurate. These speakers' first language may strongly influence their pronunciation, as well as their vocabulary and syntax when they attempt to personalize their utterances. Frequent misunderstandings may arise but, with repetition or rephrasing, Novice-High speakers can generally be understood by sympathetic interlocutors used to non-natives. When called on to handle simply a variety of topics and perform functions pertaining to the Intermediate level, a Novice-High speaker can sometimes respond in intelligible sentences, but will not be able to sustain sentence-level discourse.

NOVICE MID
Speakers at the Novice-Mid level communicate minimally and with difficulty by using a number of isolated words and memorized phrases limited by the particular context in which the language has been learned. When responding to direct questions, they may utter only two or three words at a time or an occasional stock answer. They pause frequently as they search for simple vocabulary or attempt to recycle their own and their interlocutor's words. Because of hesitations, lack of vocabulary, inaccuracy, or failure to respond appropriately, Novice-Mid speakers may be understood with great difficulty even by sympathetic interlocutors accustomed to dealing with non-natives. When called on to handle topics by performing functions associated with the Intermediate level, they frequently resort to repetition, words from their native language, or silence.

NOVICE LOW
Speakers at the Novice-Low level have no real functional ability and, because of their pronunciation, they may be unintelligible. Given adequate time and familiar cues, they may be able to exchange greetings, give their identity, and name a number of familiar objects from their immediate environment. They are unable to perform functions or handle topics pertaining to the Intermediate level, and cannot therefore participate in a true conversational exchange.

the levels. In addition to interviewer questions, the test can contain a number of role-plays between the interviewer and the examinee.

The ACTFL scale is a **behavioural rating scale**, in that it describes features of learner language in specific contexts of language use (Brindley, 1998). This is in contrast to **theory-derived analytic scales**, which stem from a model of communicative competence and describe degrees of language ability without reference to specific situations. Behavioural speaking scales usually describe different kinds of tasks that the learners can handle at the different levels and the degree of skill with which they can handle them. They thus describe performance, but the score interpretations are usually related to the underlying competence of the examinees.

The detail of the ACTFL scale makes the descriptors quite concrete, but as a whole the scale is long. It is difficult to conceptualise from one, two, or even five readings. The interviewers are trained in a 5-day workshop, and they only become qualified after post-training practice interviews. As a behavioural rating scale, it has been criticised because the evidence for its effectiveness comes from the test itself rather than independent theoretical or empirical rationales for the ordering of tasks and language features on the scale (e.g. Lantolf and Frawley, 1985; Bachman and Savignon, 1986; Kramsch, 1986; Bachman, 1990). Its advantages include that, since its introduction in 1986, teachers and learners in the US have clearly started to pay attention to language use instead of language knowledge.

The Test of Spoken English scale

The Test of Spoken English (TSE) scale (ETS, 2001b) is a combination of holistic and analytic rating scales. **Analytic scales** contain a number of criteria, usually 3–5, each of which has descriptors at the different levels of the scale. The scale forms a grid, and the examinees usually get a profile of scores, one for each of the criteria. The advantages of analytic scales include the detailed guidance that they give to raters, and the rich information that they provide on specific strengths and weaknesses in examinee performances.

The TSE scale has five levels, which are labelled 20, 30, 40, 50 and 60. There are three versions of the TSE scale. The administrator-oriented, concise scale only describes communication ability in one sentence per level. These statements are in bold in Table 4.3. The next degree of detail is intended for examinees and the general public. Four additional statements per level describe the examinees' functional competence, sociolinguistic competence, discourse competence and linguistic competence. The most detailed version of the scale is mainly intended for raters who are learning to use the scale. It contains descriptions of what the examinee language is like at the different bands. As an example, the detailed band descriptors for Overall features are given in Table 4.4.

The differences between the levels in the first two versions of the scale are based on quantifiers like 'generally effective' and 'somewhat effective'. The categories indicate that it is a theory-derived analytic scale.

Table 4.3 *The Test of Spoken English rating scale (ETS, 2001b: 29)*

60	**Communication almost always effective: task performed very competently.**
	Functions performed clearly and effectively
	Appropriate response to audience/situation
	Coherent, with effective use of cohesive devices
	Use of linguistic features almost always effective; communication not affected by minor errors
50	**Communication generally effective: task performed competently.**
	Functions generally performed clearly and effectively
	Generally appropriate response to audience/situation
	Coherent, with some effective use of cohesive devices
	Use of linguistic features generally effective; communication generally not affected by errors
40	**Communication somewhat effective: task performed somewhat competently.**
	Functions performed somewhat clearly and effectively
	Somewhat appropriate response to audience/situation
	Somewhat coherent, with some use of cohesive devices
	Use of linguistic features somewhat effective; communication sometimes affected by errors
30	**Communication generally not effective: task generally performed poorly.**
	Functions generally performed unclearly and ineffectively
	Generally inappropriate response to audience/situation
	Generally incoherent, with little use of cohesive devices
	Use of linguistic features generally poor; communication often impeded by major errors
20	**No effective communication: no evidence of ability to perform task.**
	No evidence that functions were performed
	No evidence of ability to respond to audience/situation
	Incoherent, with no use of cohesive devices
	Use of linguistic features poor; communication ineffective due to major errors

The model that it refers to, Bachman and Palmer's (1996) Communicative Language Ability, will be discussed in the next chapter. The most detailed version of the scale connects the model with actual descriptions of examinee language. These help raters make consistent rating decisions.

The 'tasks' and 'functions' in the scale descriptors refer to the test tasks. The TSE is a tape-mediated test of oral communication in English (ETS, 2001a). Its twelve tasks ask the examinees to perform functions such as giving directions, giving and supporting opinions, and hypothesising about future events or developments. The taped performances from all around the world are rated centrally at the test program office at ETS. The twelve responses are scored one by one, and the final score for an

Table 4.4 *The Test of Spoken English band descriptors for Overall features (ETS, 2001b: 30)*

---

60   **Communication almost always effective: task performed very competently.**
Speaker volunteers information freely, with little or no effort, and may go beyond the task by using additional appropriate functions.
- Native-like repair strategies
- Sophisticated expressions
- Very strong content
- Almost no listener effort required

50   **Communication generally effective: task performed competently.**
Speaker volunteers information, sometimes with effort; usually does not run out of time.
- Linguistic weaknesses may necessitate some repair strategies that may be slightly distracting
- Expressions sometimes awkward
- Generally strong content
- Little listener effort required

40   **Communication somewhat effective: task performed somewhat competently.**
Speaker responds with effort; sometimes provides limited speech sample and sometimes runs out of time.
- Sometimes excessive, distracting, and ineffective repair strategies used to compensate for linguistic weaknesses (e.g. vocabulary and/or grammar)
- Adequate content
- Some listener effort required

30   **Communication generally not effective: task generally performed poorly.**
Speaker responds with much effort; provides limited speech sample and often runs out of time.
- Repair strategies excessive, very distracting, and ineffective
- Much listener effort required
- Difficult to tell if task is fully performed because of linguistic weaknesses, but function can be identified

20   **No effective communication: no evidence of ability to perform task.**
Extreme speaker effort is evident; speaker may repeat prompt, give up on task, or be silent.
- Attempts to perform task end in failure
- Only isolated words or phrases intelligible, even with much listener effort
- Function cannot be identified

---

examinee is an average of the task scores, rounded to the nearest 5 (20, 25, 30, 35, etc.).

The Common European Framework speaking scales

The *Common European Framework of Reference* (CEF) (Council of Europe, 2001) is a resource for language education. It is intended to help learners, teachers and assessors set goals for language learning and give them support to reach them. As a part of this, it contains a range of 'illustrative descriptors' of language ability, including some for speaking. The descriptors have not been developed for any particular test, but they can be used as a basis for creating test-specific criteria. When doing this, it would be useful to analyse some learner performances at different levels in the intended test situation to see if the descriptors correspond to them and if some more descriptions can be added, probably in the concrete style of the most detailed TSE scale.

Two types of scales in the CEF that have not yet been exemplified in this chapter are analytic criteria that focus on linguistic features (Table 4.5), and task-specific scales (Table 4.6). Like most of the CEF scales, these have six levels: two at Basic (A1 and A2), two at Independent (B1 and B2), and two at Proficient (C1 and C2).

Since it has five criteria, the scale in Table 4.5 is analytic, and given that it describes what the learners actually do, it is a behavioural rating scale. The descriptors have been written for general rather than specific purposes, so that if it were used in a professionally specific speaking assessment, say French for business, the functions and language-use contexts would have to be modified to suit that test. While the criteria focus on language, they do so from the perspective of interactive communication. The Interaction scale provides some concrete suggestions for wordings when rating interactive skills, while for tasks that require long turns by a single speaker the Coherence scale may provide some useful concepts. If this scale were used to rate performances on a speaking test, the developers would have to decide whether the examinees should get five analytic scores, a combination of them as an overall score, or both. They would also have to specify rules for deriving the overall score. The decisions would depend on the purpose for which they are using the test.

The scale in Table 4.6 is clearly delimited to a specific kind of talk. It only covers the lower end of the CEF scale because the expectation is that,

Table 4.5 *Analytic descriptors of spoken language (Council of Europe, 2001: 28–29)*

	Range	Accuracy	Fluency	Interaction	Coherence
C2	Shows great flexibility reformulating ideas in differing linguistic forms to convey finer shades of meaning precisely, to give emphasis, to differentiate and to eliminate ambiguity. Also has a good command of idiomatic expressions and colloquialisms.	Maintains consistent grammatical control of complex language, even while attention is otherwise engaged (e.g. in forward planning, in monitoring others' reactions).	Can express him/herself spontaneously at length with a natural colloquial flow, avoiding or backtracking around any difficulty so smoothly that the interlocutor is hardly aware of it.	Can interact with ease and skill, picking up and using non-verbal and intonational cues apparently effortlessly. Can interweave his/her contribution into the joint discourse with fully natural turntaking, referencing, allusion making, etc.	Can create coherent and cohesive discourse making full and appropriate use of a variety of organisational patterns and a wide range of connectors and other cohesive devices.
C1	Has a good command of a broad range of language allowing him/her to select a reformulation to express him/herself clearly in an appropriate style on a wide range of general, academic, professional or leisure topics without having to restrict what he/she wants to say.	Consistently maintains a high degree of grammatical accuracy; errors are rare, difficult to spot and generally corrected when they do occur.	Can express him/herself fluently and spontaneously, almost effortlessly. Only a conceptually difficult subject can hinder a natural, smooth flow of language.	Can select a suitable phrase from a readily available range of discourse functions to preface his remarks in order to get or to keep the floor and to relate his/her own contributions skilfully to those of other speakers.	Can produce clear, smoothly flowing, well-structured speech, showing controlled use of organisational patterns, connectors and cohesive devices.

	Range	Accuracy	Fluency	Interaction	Coherence
B2	Has a sufficient range of language to be able to give clear descriptions and express viewpoints on most general topics, without much conspicuous searching for words, using some complex sentence forms to do so.	Shows a relatively high degree of grammatical control. Does not make errors which cause misunderstanding, and can correct most of his/her mistakes.	Can produce stretches of language with fairly even tempo: although he/she can be hesitant as he/she searches for patterns and expressions. There are a few noticeably long pauses.	Can initiate discourse, take his/her turn when appropriate and end conversation when he/she needs to, though he/she may not always do this elegantly. Can help the discussion along on familiar ground confirming comprehension, inviting others in, etc.	Can use a limited number of cohesive devices to link his/her utterances into clear, coherent discourse, though there may be some 'jumpiness' in a long contribution.
B1	Has enough language to get by, with sufficient vocabulary to express him/herself with some hesitation and circumlocutions on topics such as family, hobbies and interests, work, travel, and current events.	Uses reasonably accurately a repertoire of frequently used 'routines' and patterns associated with more predictable situations.	Can keep going comprehensibly, even though pausing for grammatical and lexical planning and repair is very evident, especially in longer stretches of free production.	Can initiate, maintain and close simple face-to-face conversations on topics that are familiar or of personal interest. Can repeat back part of what someone has said to confirm mutual understanding.	Can link a series of shorter, discrete simple elements into a connected, linear sequence of points.

Table 4.5 (*cont.*)

	Range	Accuracy	Fluency	Interaction	Coherence
A2	Uses basic sentence patterns with memorised phrases, groups of a few words and formulae in order to communicate limited information in simple everyday situations.	Uses some simple structures correctly, but still systematically makes basic mistakes.	Can make him/herself understood in very short utterances, even though pauses, false starts and reformulation are very evident.	Can answer questions and respond to simple statements. Can indicate when he/she is following but is rarely able to understand enough to keep conversation going of his/her own accord.	Can link groups of words with simple connectors like 'and' and 'but' and 'because'.
A1	Has a very basic repertoire of words and simple phrases related to personal details and particular concrete situations.	Shows only limited control of a few simple grammatical structures and sentence patterns in a memorised repertoire.	Can manage very short, isolated, mainly pre-packaged utterances, with much pausing to search for expressions, to articulate less familiar words, and to repair communication.	Can ask and answer questions about personal details. Can interact in a simple way but communication is totally dependent on repetition, rephrasing and repair.	Can link words or groups of words with very basic linear connectors like 'and' or 'then'.

Table 4.6 *A task-specific scale for goal-oriented co-operation (e.g. repairing a car, discussing a document, organising an event) (Council of Europe, 2001: 79)*

C2	As B2
C1	As B2
B2	Can understand detailed instructions reliably.
	Can help along the progress of the work by inviting others to join in, say what they think, etc.
	Can outline an issue or a problem clearly, speculating about causes or consequences, and weighing advantages and disadvantages of different approaches.
B1	Can follow what is said, though he/she may occasionally have to ask for repetition or clarification if the other people's talk is rapid or extended.
	Can explain why something is a problem, discuss what to do next, compare and contrast alternatives.
	Can give brief comments on the views of others.
	Can generally follow what is said and, when necessary, can repeat back part of what someone has said to confirm mutual understanding.
	Can make his/her opinions and reactions understood as regards possible solutions or the question of what to do next, giving brief reasons and explanations.
	Can invite others to give their views on how to proceed.
A2	Can understand enough to manage simple, routine tasks without undue effort, asking very simply for repetition when he/she does not understand.
	Can discuss what to do next, making and responding to suggestions, asking for and giving directions.
	Can indicate when he/she is following and can be made to understand what is necessary, if the speaker takes the trouble.
	Can communicate in simple and routine tasks using simple phrases to ask for and provide things, to get simple information and to discuss what to do next.
A1	Can understand questions and instructions addressed carefully and slowly to him/her and follow short, simple directions.
	Can ask people for things, and give people things.

in this type of task, the higher three levels cannot be reliably distinguished from each other in terms of *what* the learner can do. Each level descriptor contains several statements. If this scale were used to rate actual performances, the developers would need to decide whether the examinees needed to show evidence of all, most, or some of the functions to be awarded a particular level.

The Melbourne medical students' diagnostic speaking scales

All the above examples include verbal definitions of the scale levels. This example is different in that there are several analytic scales, but the scale levels are only defined by numbers.

The diagnostic speaking test for medical undergraduates at Melbourne University (Grove and Brown, 2001) is used to identify students who need support with their communication skills. From their first year of study onwards, the students have to communicate with patients in clinical practice sessions and work collaboratively in small-group activities. The test was developed to provide detailed feedback to both native and non-native speaker students to help them cope with the demands of their studies.

The performances on the test are rated on two sets of criteria, one language-oriented and the other task-specific. The criteria in this example are related to an informal discussion task on the topic of education. The examinees present and justify their opinions about it and discuss them with the examiner.

The scales in Table 4.7 are **numerical rating scales** (Linn and Gronlund, 1995), where the scales have titles, but the levels of each scale are only identified by numbers. This is useful when the raters can be expected to agree about the meaning of the numbers. However, the interpretations of the scores usually vary across raters because numbers in this sense are vague. When there is an even number of levels, as in this example, the raters need to decide whether the examinee is on the weak or strong side of the middle point of each scale. The alternative is to have an odd number, but the difficulty with that solution is that the interpretation of the middle score may be particularly variable – very broad for some raters and rather narrow for others. This format of scales is therefore not very common in speaking assessment. More informative rating scales describe how students behave at each of the score levels, as in the earlier scale examples in this chapter. This gives a basis for greater rater agreement and more informative feedback.

In the case of the Melbourne medical students' test, the raters have access to detailed descriptions of the meaning of each scale during the rating process. This includes examples of the kinds of communication behaviour that the criteria mean (Grove and Brown, 2001). Unfortunately, these descriptions have not been published. Nevertheless, this format is probably useful in situations like this, where new rating concepts are being explored. The scales can be written out once the test has been used

Table 4.7 *Task-specific numerical scales for an informal discussion task (Adapted from Grove and Brown, 2001)*

Task 2: Informal discussion

Adequacy of participation

| Maintenance of interaction | 6 | 5 | 4 | 3 | 2 | 1 |
| Initiative, expansiveness | 6 | 5 | 4 | 3 | 2 | 1 |

Quality of ideas

| Maturity and quality of thought | 6 | 5 | 4 | 3 | 2 | 1 |

Interpersonal skills

| Engagement, rapport | 6 | 5 | 4 | 3 | 2 | 1 |
| Nonverbal behaviour | 6 | 5 | 4 | 3 | 2 | 1 |

Coherence and expression

| Clarity of ideas | 6 | 5 | 4 | 3 | 2 | 1 |
| Cohesion and coherence | 6 | 5 | 4 | 3 | 2 | 1 |

Register and tone

Level of formality	6	5	4	3	2	1
Politeness	6	5	4	3	2	1
Directness	6	5	4	3	2	1
Tone of voice	6	5	4	3	2	1

Linguistic criteria

Language

Range of structure and vocabulary	6	5	4	3	2	1
Breadth and precision of expression	6	5	4	3	2	1
Accuracy	6	5	4	3	2	1

Production

Pronunciation	6	5	4	3	2	1
Intonation, stress and rhythm	6	5	4	3	2	1
Voice quality	6	5	4	3	2	1

for some time so that performances at different levels can be analysed for key features.

Regarding the rating concepts used in this example, the task-related criteria of 'adequacy of participation', 'quality of ideas' and 'interpersonal skills' are broader than usual for language tests. The tasks and criteria were developed together with the score users – medical educators at Melbourne University – and these were the kinds of concepts that they found important in the situations that the students meet outside the test. As this was what the scores were intended to be relevant to, the test developers defined the rating criteria accordingly.

A diagnostic rating checklist for a description task

Instead of using undefined numerical scales, test developers and raters can also give diagnostic ratings through **rating checklists**. These are detailed lists of features that can be used to describe successful performances on a task. A successful performance may not always have all of these features, but it will have many of them, and when raters are provided with a list of these they can make a quick note of which features they can see in a performance they are observing and which are noticeably missing. An example of a rating checklist is shown in Table 4.8. This checklist was developed for rating a description task where the interlocutor asks the examinee to describe the room or area where they work. The task will be discussed in more detail in Chapter 7.

Two types of checklist are used in this example. The first is a yes/no format. For each feature on the list, the rater ticks whether it was present in the performance or not. The space for comments can be used to note what was particularly good or bad about each aspect of the description. The second is a +/− format. The rater marks strengths with a plus sign and weaknesses with a minus sign, and possibly writes down some quick comments. The more concrete these notes are, for example quotes of phrases or sounds that the examinee used, the more useful the notes are going to be when giving feedback to the speakers. For helping examinees learn more, comments on weaknesses are particularly useful, while comments on strengths make them more aware of their skills and help them feel good about their language learning.

Since rating checklists contain long lists of aspects of task performance, they can only be developed when the designers know the tasks

Table 4.8 *A rating checklist for a workplace description task*

Content and structure of description

	Yes	No	Comment
Mentions what he/she does for a living	❏	❏	
Says where the workplace is	❏	❏	
Describes location of room or area	❏	❏	
Describes the room/area itself	❏	❏	
Identifies the key tools and activities	❏	❏	
Describes atmosphere/feelings	❏	❏	

Language of description

+/−		Comment
	Flow of speech	
	Rhythm and speed	
	Pronunciation	
	Intonation	
	Stress	
	Hesitation	
	Vocabulary range	
	Filler words	
	Grammar	
	Other, what?	

and performances very well. In practice, this means analysing learners' and experts' performances on the tasks with a view to describing what makes the performances successful. Checklists are useful for giving diagnostic feedback, but the degree of their usefulness depends on the perceptiveness of the features on the list.

Rating checklists are essentially diagnostic and descriptive. They can be used simply as they are, as in Table 4.8, but often they are used together with rating scales. Checklists that specify content and structure of talk, as in the first half of Table 4.8, make raters focus on task achievement and task-specific features of communication. Language-oriented checklists, as in the second half, are more generic. Thus, the developers can choose to use checklists with either task-specific or holistic scales, depending on the purpose of their test.

Concerns in developing speaking scales

How many levels?

The number of levels that a scale will have is one of the central questions in scale development. The more levels there are, the more specific the feedback will be, and the easier it will be to show progress, for example from the beginning to the end of a semester of language classes. However, since scales are also about measurement, it is important to ask how many levels the raters can distinguish consistently. An easy way of checking this is to see how well raters agree with themselves when they rate the same performances twice, with a week's interval between ratings, for example. Another check might be to see how well two raters agree with each other. Usually the answer is that the lower the number of levels, the more consistent the decisions. The compromise is some-where in the middle, and test-specific scales often have four to six levels. To get the best of both worlds, a school might decide to use two types of scales, one for reporting progress in foreign language learning across terms and years, and another for grading performances on individual tests.

How many criteria?

The examples in this chapter included holistic and analytic scales. If the decision is made to use analytic rating criteria, the developers need to decide how many criteria there will be. The *Common European Framework* (Council of Europe, 2001: 193) suggests that four or five categories begin to cause a cognitive load for raters and seven is a psycholog-ical upper limit. Since it is also important that the analytic criteria are conceptually independent, at least to some extent, five to six criteria may be close to the maximum. However, grouping the criteria under concep-tual headings, as in the last example, may enable raters to make more detailed ratings, which is useful for diagnostic purposes.

What should the level definitions say?

The scales in all but the last example in this chapter contained verbal def-initions of the levels. These guide the raters to rate the performances consistently, and they also explain the meaning of the scores to the examinees and score users. Because of this connection with score meaning, the scales are closely related to the construct definition of the test. They are also directly linked to the tasks, because to be useful they need to describe the kinds of speaking skills that the tasks reveal. The construct, the tasks and the criteria thus need to be developed together.

To be useful, the scale descriptors need to be concrete. However, they also need to be practical. If they are very long, it is difficult to memorise the scale and use it consistently. Also, if the descriptors are very detailed, it is difficult to find performances that exhibit all the features described, and then the raters need to decide which of two or three possible levels should be awarded. Undefined levels, or scales with only evaluative labels such as a range from 'excellent' to 'poor', on the other hand, cause difficulties because of their vagueness. They may be practical if there is only one rater, but only if he or she is internally consistent. This is why some verbal definition of levels is usually better than none.

To develop good, clear and concrete level descriptors, the developers need to listen to examinee performances at different levels and describe what it is that makes them a certain level. This usually takes more than one iteration of drafting, tryout and revision. Scale development methods are discussed later in this chapter.

Norm-referenced or criterion-referenced?

The contrast between **norm-referenced** and **criterion-referenced** scores has to do with the way the scores are interpreted. If the performances are compared against some external criterion, such as the ability to perform a certain job, the interpretation is criterion-referenced. A set of level definitions that describe learner language can also constitute a criterion against which performances are assessed. If learner performances are compared against each other or against standards set by some norming group, for example sixth-graders at the end of the school year, the scores are norm-referenced.

In practice, especially in school-based tests, criterion-referenced and norm-referenced score interpretations form a continuum, but it is usually possible to say which orientation is closer to the intended application of a scale. Many speaking scores are criterion-referenced or at least close to the criterion-referenced end of the continuum. Many grading systems at schools are close to the norm-referenced end of the continuum, because the assessments are made against the expected performance of learners at a particular grade.

Methods of developing scales for assessing speaking

When developing a speaking test, it might be attractive to adopt an existing scale, possibly one that is used by a formal examination body, and take it on trust that it is appropriate, useful, and well developed. However, scales must always be related to the purpose of the test and the definition of the construct to be assessed. Moreover, many existing scales have been developed through intuitive methods, without systematic analysis of quantitative or qualitative data (Council of Europe, 2001: 207). Even if existing scales were used as a basis, it would therefore be a good idea to modify them using some of the empirical analyses discussed below (for more extensive discussion of scale development, see Council of Europe, 2001: 205–216). The methods also apply when creating original rating scales.

The basic rules for writing good skill-level descriptors are like those for writing any good public texts. The rules should be brief, clear, definite, and comprehensible independently, without reference to other descriptors (Council of Europe, 2001: 205–207). Brevity makes scales user-friendly both for people who are reading a scale for the first time and for assessors, who may use the scale as a reference during the assessment process. Clarity means the absence of jargon. Simple wordings and sentence structures help readers understand the descriptors more quickly and easily. Definiteness comes from being concrete, for example by naming tasks that learners at each level can do and describing the way they sound when they do them. An example of an unsuccessful criterion is 'Can use a range of appropriate strategies' (Council of Europe, 2001:206). On the face of it, this descriptor may seem acceptable, but what exactly does 'strategies' refer to, what do they need to be 'appropriate' to, and what does 'a range' mean? Each reader may have his or her own answers. Qualifiers like *a few, many,* and *most* or *limited, moderate* and *good* are particular cases in point. In later stages of scale development, especially now that the work is often done on computer, it is attractive to replace one qualifier with another when describing the next level up. However, only concrete descriptions or examples will help assessors keep the levels apart consistently. Definite formulations will also support descriptor independence, so that readers will not need to read the adjacent descriptors to understand what a particular descriptor means.

The lowest levels on rating scales are often worded negatively, as it is easier to say what learners at these levels cannot do than what they can do. In principle, if the aim of a rating scale is simply to get assessors to agree, negative formulations may serve the purpose just as well as positive ones. However, if the criteria are shared with the learners and especially if they are used as descriptions of learning goals, positive formulations are likely to serve the purpose better. Sometimes this can be achieved by focusing on what the learners *can* do with their limited language, such as dealing with predictable everyday situations or naming basic objects, places, and qualities such as colour and size. Sometimes it may help to add qualifiers to positive descriptors, such as in the descriptor for level B1 in spoken fluency in the CEF: 'Can keep going comprehensibly, even though pausing for grammatical and lexical planning and repair is very evident, especially in longer stretches of free production' (Council of Europe 2001: 129). When working on scale descriptors, it is important to consider the audiences for different scales, and sometimes it is necessary to re-write the scales for different audiences. This might mean simply saying more to some audiences than to others, as in the TSE example above, or using technical concepts with audiences such as raters, and non-technical ones with examinees and score users.

Intuitive methods

Intuitive methods of scale development are not based on data collection but on principled interpretation of experience. The scale may be developed by one person only, or by a small committee. The developers usually have considerable experience in teaching and/or materials development with learners at relevant ability levels. In addition, the developers may consult existing scales, curriculum documents, teaching materials and other relevant source material, and then distil the information into draft descriptors at an agreed number of levels. In the smallest scale contexts, the descriptors might be revised once or twice; in broader efforts, the committee would probably meet several times and consult other experts and/or trial users of the scale in order to achieve a usable formulation of the scale with which all participants can agree, at least in broad terms. With influential institutional scales such as the ILR scale mentioned above, a similar development method to this was followed in an even longer process (Clark and Clifford, 1988). The developers came to share an understanding of the scale through repeated discussions, revisions and scale application to learner performances until the scale was stabilised and then began to be used for its intended purpose. New raters are trained in the use of the scale and their work is monitored to ensure that they, too, share an understanding of the scale.

Qualitative methods

Qualitative methods of scale development involve asking groups of experts to analyse data related to the scale. The material that they are asked to work on can be the scale level descriptors or samples of performances at different levels.

If the developers decide to work with the level descriptors, they can start simply by investigating how far a group of prospective scale users agrees with the grouping of the different statements that make up the scale. In preparation for the session, they divide the scale into its constituent statements so that each of them only describes one activity or narrowly defined level of achievement (e.g. 'Can handle very short exchanges' and 'Can use everyday polite forms of greeting and address' would be two different statements). Then, they ask the experts to rank the descriptors according to difficulty, and possibly group them into as many levels as the scale has. The result indicates which descriptors are clear to all or most users and which ones cause confusion. In the follow-up discussion, the experts can be asked to explain why they interpreted individual descriptors in a certain way and possibly identify words or phrases in the scale statements that helped or confused them. They can also be asked to suggest revisions to the wordings. Moreover, the scale developers might want to reject descriptors over which experts could not agree. This method represents an empirical approach to consensus-building, and it is the way in which the descriptor pool for the CEF was developed (see e.g. North, 1996/2000).

Another approach to sharing understandings of levels is to use performance samples. If a scale already exists, the experts can work on samples that have been rated by several raters. The samples can be selected because of strong agreement – or disagreement – about their level. Alternatively, the experts might be asked to bring with them some test performances that they think represent the levels particularly well. In the session, the performances are analysed in order to compare the performance features with the wordings of the scales. Any discrepancies are noted and discussed, with possible notes or drafts for revisions in the scale. The speaking scales for the International English Language Testing Service (IELTS) test were developed in this way (Alderson, 1991). Since speaking test performances need to be observed from audio or video tapes, the process can be somewhat time-consuming, but it may be possible to facilitate it by observing the whole performances only once or twice and using judiciously selected 2–3 minute extracts after that. Even if the experts soon learn to remember the performances, the approach should not be reduced to memory-based rationalisation, however. It is important to actually observe and analyse the performances and create or modify the descriptors on that basis.

If the sample performances have not been rated before the analysis begins, both the rating and the writing of descriptors can be done at the same time. In one variant of this approach, the raters are first asked to rate a set of performances on a numerical scale that has the desired number of levels and then to tell the developers why they gave the ratings they did. The comments are most detailed and concrete if the scale constructors ask each of the raters to review the performances again and stop the tape whenever they hear something that makes the performance belong to a certain level. The phrases that the raters use for describing each level are then collected and used for scale development (Brown *et al.*, 2001). In another variant, the experts do not start with a scale. Instead, they divide a set of performances into smaller and smaller groups and discuss the features that distinguish them. They first divide the whole set of performances into two groups, lower and higher. Then they do this again with the two sub-groups, and possibly once more with the still smaller groups, depending on how many levels there need to be in the scale. The features that the raters mention are incorporated into the draft level descriptors, and some whole performances are then rated and analysed to check how well the draft descriptors work and whether they describe the performances at the different levels with any accuracy. Alternatively, the raters might be asked to compare a pair of performances at a time, stating which one is better and why. Notes are again written about the features that the raters mention, and these are used as material for scale level descriptors (Pollitt and Murray, 1996).

Quantitative methods

Quantitative methods of scale development require a fair amount of statistical expertise. This is usually most readily available in large testing or research institutions, although individual teachers or testers may of course also have the skills that are needed. The questions addressed in quantitative studies usually have to do with scale validation. They may involve combining qualitative and quantitative research techniques, and possibly require the gathering of large data sets.

One quantitative design was used by Fulcher (1996) when he developed a rating scale for fluency. He first conducted a discourse analysis of a set of performances and counted the occurrence of a range of fluency features in them, and then he used multiple regression to determine which of the features were significant in determining the examinee scores. These features were then used to construct level descriptors. While time-consuming, the advantage of this technique was that the resulting scale was firmly based on data rather than rationalised experience, and in a follow-up study Fulcher showed that raters were able to use the scale consistently to rate a set of new performances. I will discuss Fulcher's scale in more detail later in this chapter.

In another research design, Chalhoub-Deville (1995) asked trained and untrained raters to rate the speaking performance of six learners of Arabic on an analytic scoring protocol. She then used multidimensional scaling and linear regression to determine which features were salient to each of the rater groups. The study showed that different rater groups valued the spoken performances differently, raising questions about whose criteria should count, and whether test scores correspond to non-tester perceptions of learner proficiency.

An advanced quantitative approach for developing or refining assessment scales is item response theory (IRT). It is a development of probability theory, and while it is most often used in language testing for placing items on a scale of difficulty, it can also be applied for placing descriptors on a scale of proficiency. There are a range of IRT models that researchers and test developers can choose from, depending on their needs and the availability of data. The most simple and robust model is named after the Danish mathematician George Rasch. This model was used when scaling the descriptors of the CEF. In a slightly different context, Milanovic *et al.* (1996) used the Rasch model to examine how clearly raters were able to distinguish the different bands of a speaking scale from each other. While the application of IRT models is very useful for language testing, the disadvantage is that it requires sizable sets of data, which are rarely available except in the most widely used tests, or in research settings.

Research on the progression of speaking ability

In this final section of this chapter, I will summarise some language testing and SLA research on the progression of speaking ability. This can support the construction of rating scales for speaking. The discussion is organised in terms of the features of talk that the studies focus on. I begin with fluency, a central if difficult concept in assessing speaking. Since this is related to pragmatic ability, I will continue with that topic. Finally, I will briefly discuss results of studies on learner grammar.

Fluency

Here is an example of a fluency scale.

Table 4.9 *The Test of English for Educational Purposes fluency scale (Weir, 1993: 44)*

0	Utterances halting, fragmentary and incoherent.
1	Utterances hesitant and often incomplete except in a few stock remarks and responses. Sentences are, for the most part, disjointed and restricted in length.
2	Signs of developing attempts at using cohesive devices, especially conjunctions. Utterances may still be hesitant, but are gaining in coherence, speed, and length.
3	Utterances, whilst occasionally hesitant, are characterized by an evenness and flow, hindered, very occasionally, by groping, rephrasing and circumlocutions. Inter-sentential connectors are used effectively as fillers.

Here is another example, with some more concrete description of learner language.

Table 4.10 *A data-based fluency scale (Hasselgren, 1998; based on Fulcher, 1996)*

1	Speakers' utterances are short, often a single word. There are long pauses when they are trying to understand the interlocutor, get clarification, or search for words or forms. Repetitions and restarts are common. Sometimes the speakers are unable to make a response, and messages are sometimes abandoned because of language shortcomings.
2	Speakers frequently need help in order to understand their interlocutor, but messages, once started, are generally fulfilled in a simplistic way, without expansion, e.g. through examples. Pausing still occurs when looking for lexical or

Table 4.10 (*cont.*)

grammatical choice – sometimes with circumlocutions and often with midway switch of formulation.

3   Speakers usually understand the interlocutor. They seem more aware of the proposition, and spend time planning this. Appropriacy of word choice becomes more important, and pausing will occur in making these choices, with some appealing to the interlocutor. Utterances tend to be more expanded. Back-channelling – using *hm* or *yeah* – helps to make conversation more natural.

4   Misunderstandings are rare. Speakers use hedges to express lack of certainty in the propositions. Few single-word utterances are given, and speakers expand their utterances, e.g. providing back-ups to opinions. Time is spent planning the content of the proposition and how exactly to express themselves and present their views. Reformulations occur when the speaker is not satisfied with the proposition or the correctness of the formulation.

5   Speakers demonstrate more confidence and are less likely to express propositional uncertainty. They rarely pause for reasons of grammar or word choice. Reformulations occur mainly for reasons of expressing proposition fully. They expand and support themselves. They respond very quickly.

Fluency is a thorny issue in assessing speaking. This is partly because the word 'fluency' has a general meaning, as in 'she is fluent in five languages', and a technical meaning when applied linguists use it to characterise a learner's speech. However, even in technical terminology, fluency can be used in a range of senses. The narrowest definitions only include a few features, typically pausing, hesitations and speech rate, whereas the broadest uses are virtually synonymous with 'speaking proficiency'. Unless the term is defined explicitly, it is simply not clear what a speaker or a writer means by it (Freed, 1995; Fulcher, 1996). Esser (1995), for example, found that when no verbal description of fluency was given to raters, they tended to disagree with each other about both the definitions they gave to it and the way they rated it when they were asked to pick the more fluent of a set of pairs of speech samples.

Definitions of fluency often include references to flow or smoothness, rate of speech, absence of excessive pausing, absence of disturbing hesitation markers, length of utterances, and connectedness (Koponen, 1995). These characterisations are complex, however, because they are not simply descriptions of a speaker's speech but also of a listener's perception of it. To illustrate this, in the phrase 'excessive pausing', the pausing is a feature of a learner's speech, while the excessiveness is based on a listener's judgement.

One central part of fluency is related to temporal aspects of speech, such as speaking rate, speech–pause relationships, and frequency of dysfluency markers such as hesitations, repetitions and self-corrections. These can be evaluated by machine and by human impression. Both kinds of studies indicate that when speakers become more fluent their speech rate increases and the speech flow contains fewer pauses and hesitations (Lennon, 1990; Freed, 1995). They also pause at semantically sensible places, which listeners perceive as the speakers' planning the content of what they are saying rather than groping for words. More fluent speakers tend to speak more and their phrases are longer. This is the way in which the levels in the first fluency scale above differ from each other (see Table 4.9).

Dissatisfied with the summary descriptions of fluency in existing rating scales, Fulcher (1993, 1996) wanted to create more concrete descriptions for it. He analysed some speech samples, summarised rater interpretations of them, and drafted a new scale of fluency. His descriptors ended up being long, more than 200 words for each level. However, at least in a research setting, raters found them informative, and they were able to use the scale consistently to rate a new set of performances (Fulcher, 1996). A summarised version of Fulcher's scale was presented in Table 4.8 above.

In addition to time-bound speed and pausing phenomena, fluency is related to the way that speakers use words, and in particular 'smallwords' such as *really*, *I mean* and *oh* (Hasselgren, 1998). To focus on the more lexical aspects of fluency, Hasselgren (1998: 155) defined it as 'the ability to contribute to what a listener, proficient in the language, would normally perceive as coherent speech, which can be understood without undue strain, and is carried out at a comfortable pace, not being disjointed or disrupted by excessive hesitation'. She suggested that smallwords are significant in this because they help speakers produce relevant turns and understand the relevance of other speakers' contributions. She summarises the tasks of smallwords in the following list:

1 They express the communicative intention of the speaker, with respect to what is to be communicated and how it affects the interactional roles of the participants
2 They point to the textual context in which an utterance has relevance
3 They indicate the cognitive effect of the previous utterance
4 They enrich the explicature of an utterance, notably by indicating degrees of commitment and vagueness
5 They indicate the state of success of the communication, acknowledging this, or appealing for confirmation, or assistance in bringing it about (Hasselgren, 1998: 167)

Studying three groups of 15–16-year-old pupils in English and Norwegian schools, Hasselgren (1998) found that the native speakers clearly used smallwords more frequently than high- and low-achieving learners, and the range of the words they used was larger, especially in mid-turn. The more fluent learners used smallwords in more native like ways, both in terms of frequency of use and in terms of the variety of forms used and the uses to which they put them. In other words, more fluent learners used formulaic expressions more frequently to get their talk started, keep going, orient their talk to the listener, appeal for understanding, and indicate interest, pleasure and enjoyment. They also softened their talk more appropriately rather than being very direct. Observing these features in learner talk would help construct more concrete and effective fluency scales.

Pragmatic skills

Since the rise of the communicative approach to language learning in the 1970s, learners' ability to *use* a language has been a central focus of attention. However, many of the early studies of SLA focused on learners' acquisition of syntax rather than pragmatics (Kasper, 1996). When studies on interlanguage pragmatics began to appear in the late 1980s and 1990s, most of them focused on differences between learners and native speakers rather than the development of pragmatic skills. Recently, initiatives by Kasper (1996), House (1996) and Bardovi-Harlig (1999) have begun to change this, and the early findings suggest that it is possible to distinguish and describe varying levels of control of pragmatic skills. Rather than using scales for something called 'pragmatic skills', it is more common for speaking assessments to focus on areas of it. The *Common European Framework*, for example, considers pragmatic skills to be composed of discourse and functional competence. It proposes six illustrative scales for this, entitled flexibility to circumstances, turntaking, thematic development (in a narrative), coherence and cohesion, fluency, and propositional precision (Council of Europe, 2001: 123–129). Let us now take a look at what SLA research says about the development of pragmatic skills.

House (1996) worked with the concept of **pragmatic fluency**, which she defined as 'a dialogic phenomenon that combines both pragmatic appropriateness of utterances and smooth continuity in ongoing talk' (p. 228). The concept is fairly closely related to fluency as discussed above, especially in the sense that Hasselgren (1998) used it, but whereas Hasselgren focused on 'keeping going' and 'keeping other speakers going', House particularly concentrated on smoothness of speaker transitions and the way that speakers made their talk cohere with what had been said before. She studied two groups of advanced learners of English during an advanced conversation course that focused on gambits and strategies, or discourse routines. She defined **gambits** as 'discourse lubricants, [which] are used to establish, maintain, and end contact . . . helping to cement segments of talk into a discourse' (p. 232). These include expressions like *yeah, okay, hm, listen* or *I mean* that link turns to the previous or the next one, or clarify or modify the interactional content of the current turn. By **strategies**, House meant speakers' knowledge and manipulation of inter-actional structures to reach their conversational goals, such as using topic introducers to prepare the ground for making a request, giving grounders prior to making it, and removing possible objections by using 'sweeteners' which promise to allay any negative effects if the wish is granted. The two groups in House's study practised the use of gambits and strategies on their course but, in addition, one group received explicit instruction about them. The students' progression was moni-tored at the start, in the middle and at the end of a 14-week course by giving them role-play tasks that involved requests.

House (1996) found that both groups made progress in their discourse skills during the course. They especially improved in their mastery of gambits related to turn change, i.e. building continuity from the previ-ous to the current turn, and appealing to the speaker's reactions in the next turn. The group that received explicit instruction used a more varied range of gambits and strategies at the end of the course. However, even this was much narrower than native English speakers' repertoire, indicating that pragmatic fluency is a difficult skill to acquire. By the end of the course, the explicit group used interpersonally focused gambits such as *you know* and *really* clearly more often than the implicit instruc-tion group. Both groups improved their control of discourse-initiating routines, with the explicit group making more gains in degree of natural-ness.

Somewhat surprisingly, neither group made progress in second-part, uptaking and responding moves after the conversation partner had initi-ated a somewhat face-threatening exchange that would have required softening from both parties for the conversation to proceed smoothly. Thus, this pragmatic skill seems to be difficult to acquire even for advanced learners (of English). House noted that this might be because the study focused on foreign rather than second language learners, an observation repeated by Kasper (2001). Those participants who had lived in the target language culture for an extended period of time were the strongest performers both at the beginning and at the end of the course, with the gap between them and the other learners remaining constant. Moreover, House's experiment, like others that have investigated pragmatic development, was conducted in a role-play setting, which does not necessarily exert similar social conditions for discussion as real life (Kasper, 2001). Thus, the results must be interpreted carefully.

More closely grammar-related aspects of pragmatic knowledge have received more attention in SLA research, with some useful empirical results coming out. Salsbury and Bardovi-Harlig (2000), for example, observed the appearance of modal forms in the oral production of a beginning group of learners of English in the course of a year. They found that these appeared in the learners' performances in a consistent acquisitional pattern: *maybe* appeared first, then *think*, followed by *can, will, would*, and finally, *could*. However, even if the learners knew these forms in some contexts, they did not start to use them when they needed to soften their expressions interactionally, for example when they disagreed with another speaker. Grammar knowledge did not automatically lead to the pragmatic knowledge of how to use the forms in interpersonally relevant ways. Similarly, Kärkkäinen (1992) found that low-level Finnish learners of English used expressions like *I think* and *I know* to express possibility, while advanced learners more often chose modal adverbs such as *perhaps* and modal verbs such as *might be*. Native speakers, in her data, chose modal verbs and adverbs even more frequently, however. Kärkkäinen concluded that the pragmatic meanings of explicit phrases like *I think* are easier to learn than those of modal verbs or other syntactic forms, even if native speakers frequently use them in these senses. Ability to use modal verbs as softeners thus indicates a high level of pragmatic knowledge in English. It might be possible to find similar indicators for pragmatic skills in other languages as well.

Learner grammar

Almost all speaking criteria make some reference to grammar, either as a part of holistic descriptors or in a separate analytic rating criterion. For example, all the ACTFL descriptors mentioned the grammatical features of the learners' speech at different levels, and the CEF analytic grid included a separate criterion called 'Accuracy'. Research also indicates that raters tend to pay a lot of attention to grammar even if the test uses several analytic criteria (Brown, 2000; McNamara, 1996).

Much of the work on common learning orders in SLA has focused on grammar. While there have been arguments in the past about whether common learning orders can be explained by nature or nurture, and whether early language learning is qualitatively different from the learning of languages later in life, most recent theories propose that people's language learning is usage-based. In other words, all language learning can ultimately be explained by the frequency with which we hear and see different language-use patterns. Ellis (2002), for instance, summarises studies from a wide range of areas including phonology, reading, spelling, lexis, morphosyntax and formulaic language, which show that the more exposure learners have had to patterns in these areas, the better they know them. This approach proposes that the processes governing language learning are universal, but it also suggests that there is inherent variation in individual language users' proficiencies due to their different experiences of language use. They come from different language backgrounds, they may or may not know other languages, and they are familiar with different ranges of language-use situations. In this vein, Brown (1996: 188) summarises the usage-based view of language knowledge as 'the constantly updated memory of all linguistic input and output that a particular speaker has ever produced or understood, a memory whose interconnections and saliences are constantly being changed and updated as new linguistic experiences are encountered'. For a detailed discussion of the assessment of learner grammar, see Purpura (forthcoming).

Several studies have established some fairly stable sequences of grammatical learning, whether the language is learned naturalistically or in instructed settings (Ellis, 1989). Pienemann (1998) explains this sequencing in his processability theory. He proposes that the reason why forms appear in a particular order in learners' language is that there is an implicational hierarchy of psycholinguistic processes that the learners need to acquire to be able to manipulate a language. This general processing hierarchy interacts with the structures of a particular language to predict the order of appearance of its morphological and grammatical features. The progression is presented in Table 4.11.

The progression from invariant word forms to plurals and definiteness, and past and present tense, and further to compound tenses, gender marking and agreement, followed by subject–verb agreement and

Table 4.11 *Hierarchy of grammatical processability according to Pienemann (1998)*

Hierarchy of processing procedures	L2 structure	Learner's L2 production
1. lemma access (i.e. access to content words)	Words	Invariant forms
2. the category procedure	Lexical morphemes	Plural, definiteness, past/ present tense agreement
3. the phrasal procedure	Phrasal structure such as agreement and tense	Definiteness agreement, gender markings, compound tense markings
4. the s-procedure	Word order and other interphrasal information	Subject–verb agreement, adjective agreement in predicative constructions
5. the subordinate procedure, if applicable	Main and subordinate clause relationships	Re-organization of word order in subordinate clauses

complex word order seems very familiar. It is in fact how grammar progression has been described in speaking scales for quite some time. Thus, in a sense, Pienemann's theory lends support to existing practice.

Summary

In this chapter, I have discussed the nature and development of rating scales for speaking. I started with examples, which illustrated a range of different types of scales, including verbally defined and numerical scales, and rating checklists, which essentially provide 0/1-type present–absent descriptions of performance features. I took up distinctions between holistic and analytic scales, general purpose and specific purpose scales, and theory-based and behavioural rating scales. I also discussed criterion-referenced and norm-referenced score interpretation, concluding that many speaking scales are used in a criterion-referenced sense. I pointed out that scales are always written for a purpose and an audience, and sometimes they may need to be re-written for different audiences.

Next, I presented a summary of methods for developing speaking scales. Following the *Common European Framework of Reference*, these were divided into intuitive, qualitative and quantitative methods. The best results can probably be achieved by combining all the approaches in the development of any scale.

Finally, I summarised some empirical findings from SLA and language testing research about the progression of speaking ability. The studies offered some support for describing learner speech at different levels, and perhaps more importantly some suggestions about the features of learner language that test developers should observe when they develop scales. If they actually analyse some performances and use the results to revise their scale, as suggested in the section on qualitative scale development methods, this may lead to the production of more concrete and user-friendly rating scales for speaking in the future.

In the last two chapters' discussions of tasks and scales, I have focused on research that is related to the concrete products of the test development process. In the next chapter, I will briefly summarise ways of linking practical test development work with theoretical models of language ability. This can be helpful when the developers want to explain how their test is related to the kinds of speaking that the examinees do outside the test.

CHAPTER FIVE

Theoretical models

When we develop speaking tests, we want the scores to be relevant to something outside the test. When the purpose of the test is rather general, as it is when we want to say something about the examinees' overall proficiency level, for example, we need a reference framework to help us explain what we mean by overall proficiency and how this is related to our test. One possibility is relating the test to a model of language ability. We can choose one model or several, depending on the types of explanations that we need in our testing context. In this chapter, I will discuss a range of models that can serve this purpose. I will also discuss the ways in which the models can be used in test development projects.

Models are not the only option for referencing speaking tests. Very often, learning-related assessments implement some of the goals of teaching curricula, for example. The curricula themselves may be based on a theoretical framework explicitly or implicitly, or they may be based on an eclectic combination of views about language learning. These, too, can help explain how the small sample of language that is rated during the assessment is related to the broader picture of language ability, but teaching frameworks are often not explicitly defined in coursebooks or curriculum documents. Models can be helpful for testing projects because they are usually presented in an explicit yet concise format, so that it is possible to view a test's construct definition in their light. At the same time, the definition can also be related to other frameworks such as curriculum documents, if so desired.

Communicative competence and (communicative) language ability

The concept of communicative competence was introduced into applied linguistics in reaction to highly grammar-focused theories of language competence, which analyse the nature of language as a system independently of its users. Communicative competence emphasises the users and their use of language for communication. In language classrooms, the communicative revolution led to the widespread use of authentic learning materials and communication exercises.

The models of communicative competence that are currently used in language education and assessment are largely based on Hymes's (1971, 1972) theory of language use in social life. He suggested that there are four levels of analysis in language use that are relevant for understanding regularities in people's use of language. The first level is what is *possible* in terms of language code, i.e. the grammatical level. At the next level, analysts should look at what is *feasible* for an individual to produce or comprehend in terms of time and processing constraints. The next level introduces the social and situational dimension of what is *appropriate* in various language-use situations. Finally, language use is shaped by what is *actually done*, i.e. by convention and habit – some formulations just happen to be commonly used by a community of speakers and others do not, even if they would be grammatically correct and their meaning would be interpretable. Part of the language knowledge of fully fledged users of a language is knowledge about such typical and untypical turns of phrase. In fact, Hymes proposes that each of the dimensions is governed by a set of rules of use that first language users learn, albeit mostly subconsciously. His distinctions of the social appropriacy dimension, captured in the SPEAKING mnemonic, were discussed briefly in Chapter 2.

Hymes's theory was originally proposed for analysing children's first language development, but it has been applied extensively in second and foreign language contexts ever since its introduction. Since the theory works on a high level of abstraction, it has often not been applied as such, but rather through a more concrete theoretical model. The most frequently used communicative model in language testing today is Bachman and Palmer's (1996) model of language ability, which is a further development of Bachman's (1990) Communicative Language Ability (CLA).

Bachman and Palmer (1996) consider language use as interaction between language users and their context. This is hypothesised to

Figure 5.1 Relationships between some hypothesised components of language use (Bachman and Palmer, 1996: 63)

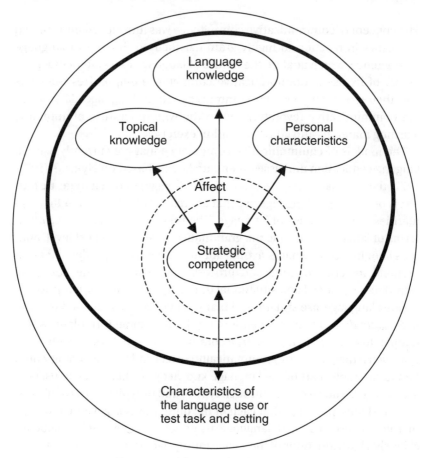

involve five components. *Language knowledge* refers to various kinds of knowledge about language in the user's memory. *Topical knowledge*, in turn, refers to the knowledge about different topics that the user brings to a language-use situation, while *personal characteristics* are basic features of the person such as sex, age and native language. In actual language use, the knowledge categories and the personal characteristics are mediated by two components, *strategic competence*, which refers to the user's metacognitive organisation and monitoring of the situation, and *affective factors*, which comprise the user's emotional responses to the situation. The relationships between the hypothesised components of language use are presented graphically in

Figure 5.1 (Bachman and Palmer, 1996: 63). While the individual language user is central in the figure, as represented by the second-largest, bold circle, the interaction between the individual and the context of language use is also drawn in.

Bachman and Palmer's (1996) notion of language ability consists of two parts, *language knowledge* and *strategic competence*. Of these, language knowledge is more componential and static, whereas strategic competence is active and dynamic. It identifies key aspects in the interactions that are taking place within an individual when he or she is interacting with the language-use setting, as illustrated in Figure 5.1. Three metacognitive components are identified under strategic competence. The first involves deciding what one is going to do, which is termed *goal-setting*, the second is evaluating the situation and one's resources to cope with it, which is termed *assessment*, and the third is deciding how to use what one has, which is termed *planning*.

Bachman and Palmer's (1996) analysis of language knowledge is based on earlier theories about communicative competence as well as empirical results from a multitrait-multimethod study (Bachman and Palmer, 1982), in which the researchers developed tasks to test grammatical, pragmatic and sociolinguistic competence through a number of test methods. They found that the results varied more clearly by the competence tested than the test method used. Grammatical competence (morphology and syntax) and pragmatic competence (vocabulary, cohesion and organisation) were closely related, whereas sociolinguistic competence (sensitivity to register, naturalness, and cultural references) was more independent. These results influenced the way that the components of language knowledge are presented (see Table 5.1).

The components of language knowledge are presented in a list-like fashion, but there are three tiers of categories in the list. The two main categories are organisational and pragmatic knowledge. Of these, organisational knowledge is focused on how utterances or sentences and texts are organised, while pragmatic knowledge concentrates on the relationship between the forms of language (utterances, sentences, texts) on the one hand and the user's communicative goals and the setting of language use on the other.

The two areas of organisational knowledge that Bachman and Palmer (1996) distinguish are grammatical knowledge, which comprises vocabulary, syntax, phonology and graphology, and textual knowledge, which comprises cohesion and rhetorical or conversational organisation. The 'functions' of functional knowledge refer to the functions that people

Table 5.1 *Areas of language knowledge (Bachman and Palmer, 1996: 68)*

Organisational knowledge
(how utterances or sentences and texts are organised)

Grammatical knowledge
(how individual utterances or sentences are organised)
Knowledge of vocabulary
Knowledge of syntax
Knowledge of phonology/graphology

Textual knowledge
(how utterances or sentences are organised to form texts)
Knowledge of cohesion
Knowledge of rhetorical or conversational organisation

Pragmatic knowledge
(how utterances or sentences and texts are related to the communicative goals of language users and to the features of the language-use setting)

Functional knowledge
(how utterances or sentences and texts are related to the communicative goals of language users)
Knowledge of ideational functions
Knowledge of manipulative functions
Knowledge of heuristic functions
Knowledge of imaginative functions

Sociolinguistic knowledge
(how utterances or sentences and texts are related to the features of the language-use setting)
Knowledge of dialects/varieties
Knowledge of registers
Knowledge of natural or idiomatic expressions
Knowledge of cultural references and figures of speech

---

accomplish through language use. Thus, the functional knowledge component follows Halliday (1976) in identifying ideational, manipulative, heuristic and imaginative functions of language use. Utterances that have an ideational function express people's experiences of the real world. Those that are used to affect the world around them have a manipulative function, while those that extend people's knowledge of the world around them have a heuristic function. The imaginative function comprises creative language use for aesthetic or humorous purposes. The sociolinguistic knowledge component focuses on the relationship between language forms and the language-use situation, consisting of the language user's knowledge of dialects and varieties, registers, natural or idiomatic expressions, and cultural references and figures of speech. This component is very close to Hymes's fourth dimension of language users' knowledge, that of knowing how the language is habitually used by the community that uses it.

Conceptually, Bachman and Palmer (1996) reject the notion of reading, writing, listening and speaking as skills, and argue that they should be seen as language use activities. Their concept of 'language knowledge' identifies components of knowledge that are relevant to all modes of language use. This does not mean that their concept of language ability is not suitable for analysing speaking assessments, but rather that the knowledges and strategies identified in the language ability model are potentially relevant in all kinds of speaking situations. Their concept of language ability is in fact highly useful as a guiding framework for speaking assessments, especially for assisting the developers with definitions of what is and what is not intended to be assessed in a particular assessment procedure. Examples of this type of use of Bachman and Palmer's model will be given in Chapter 6.

The usefulness of the language ability model and other componential models for test development rests on the usefulness of their categories. Bachman and Palmer's (1996) concept of language ability names dimensions in language use, and it helps assessment developers check how well rounded their tasks and assessment criteria are in terms of them. It views tasks as language use situations, and making test developers compare test tasks with non-test language-use tasks may be very helpful. If the tasks are too limited, perhaps another task can be added.

The main limitations of componential models of communicative competence have to do with their emphasis on the *language* characteristics of the language-use situation and their static view of communication. Admittedly, language knowledge is only one component in the big picture of language use (see Figure 5.1), but its detailed definition directs attention to it. Consequently, the other knowledge types and their interactions in communication may receive less emphasis, especially since they essentially happen inside the language user's head, outside the reach of direct observation. Inferences about the language user's metacognitive processes and emotional reactions can be made on the basis of his or her actions and introspective reports, but the model still essentially focuses on the individual language user. What this means, then, is that assessment developers might want to use Bachman and Palmer's (1996) language ability model and other frameworks in parallel.

Activity theory and sociocultural approaches to language learning

In recent years, the SLA field has seen rising interest in alternatives to individually oriented theories of language, particularly those related to sociocultural theory. Originally presented in the early 1900s by the Russian psychologist Lev Vygotsky, sociocultural theory proposes that the proper object of study for psychology is human action rather than an individual's cognition. Action and thinking are inseparable, and since action happens in society, this becomes part of the object of study. In other words, Vygotsky proposes that social interaction plays such a fundamental role in the development of human cognition that cognition should be studied as a social rather than an individual concept. Culture has a central position in sociocultural theory, and it is seen to encompass all means of human meaning-making such as arithmetic signs, music and art and, above all, language. As a set of shared habits among a community of actors, culture is considered to be as objective as the physical, chemical and biological environment. People's participation in social practices carries culture (and, with it, language) from generation to generation, and it is through participation in cultural activities that people learn language. Lantolf and Pavlenko (1998: 143) characterise the overall nature of sociocultural theory by stating that it is 'a theory of real individuals rather than idealised abstractions that approaches its objects of study much more from the hermeneutic (interpretative) and historical standpoint than it does from the traditional experimental approach to research'.

The current formulation of sociocultural theory is **activity theory** (Lantolf, 2000). As the name implies, the theory sees mental behaviour as action. It concerns all aspects of action: not just *what* the person is doing, but also *how* the person is acting with objects and/or other individuals in the social environment, *where* the person is acting, *when* the activity occurs, and *why* (or what the motives and goals underlying the activity are) (Lantolf and Pavlenko, 1998). Activities are considered significant when the individual acts purposefully in order to accomplish some goal. The focus is not on the individual but on the activity, which is analysed in terms of the individual's motives and goals as well as the culture-based rules of the activity system that the individual is following. In the sociocultural view, a speaker speaks with internalised 'voices of others'. This builds on the belief that language is culturally mediated and learned through experiences with others in direct contact or indirectly, via reading, television and film. Thinking is similarly viewed as social, as thought is considered to develop from internalised speech.

Activity theory and the sociocultural approach are conceptually highly abstract. Thus, it is difficult to implement them as reference frameworks for assessments in the same way as the developers can use communicative models such as Bachman and Palmer's (1996) language ability. However, it is important to consider their implications for assessment, not least because they challenge some current orthodoxies of assessment as an activity. The main challenge is directed at the emphasis in current assessment practices on the individual speaker. Whereas sociocultural theory considers any inter-action as joint action governed by cultural norms, the logic that underlies most modern assessments of speaking is that the examinee's performance can be evaluated in isolation. The tester is responsible for the discourse environment, which should be held as constant as possible for all examin-ees, and the examinee provides a sample of language that gets rated. While it is often recognised that the test interaction really is co-constructed (e.g., Lumley and Brown, 1997; Brown and Hill, 1998), ratings are still given to individuals, and calls are made for assessor training to improve the standar-disation of the test. One way of taking a more socioculturally appropriate approach to testing might be to allow more individualisation, both in terms of offering a selection of tasks in formal, organised tests, and in terms of taking a portfolio approach to assessment so that the participants could bring samples of their real language-use activities for assessment. On a fun-damental level, the sociocultural approach also challenges the notion of using cultural appropriateness as an assessment criterion, as examinees can only reasonably be expected to know the cultural patterns of activities that they have participated in. And, in general, activity theory highlights the fact that assessment, too, is an activity, and the participants will primarily interpret it as such. The examinees may be asked to simulate some real lan-guage-use situation, such as giving directions about how to drive some-where, or treating a patient, but since they know that they are in a test, this imposes another set of expectations and norms on the communication. This is why instructions about the kinds of strategies that earn examinees good scores are important for fairness.

Speaking as a process

The speaking-specific model that has been used in teaching and assess-ment programs is Bygate's (1987) model of speech as a process. It was in fact developed for teacher education to help teachers plan classroom activities in order to support learning. The model is more individually than socially oriented, and it views learner speech as a process.

As mentioned in Chapter 2, Bygate considers the special features of speaking to result from two sets of conditions under which people speak: processing and reciprocity. In terms of processing, speaking requires simultaneous action: 'the words are being spoken as they are being decided and as they are being understood' (p. 11). Reciprocity conditions mean that speakers have to adapt to their listeners and adjust what they say according to the listeners' reactions.

Since Bygate views speaking as a speaker-internal process, his first level of analysis is three processing stages: planning, selection and production. Under these main headings, he places the knowledge and strategy components identified in componential models. He also makes a basic distinction between knowledge and skill, knowledge being what enables learners to talk, and skill being the active component that is involved when they are actively engaged in interaction. He emphasises the importance of skill practice, but recognises that both are needed when speakers speak. A summary of Bygate's model of speaking is presented in Figure 5.2.

To enable *planning* in an interactive speaking situation, Bygate proposes that learners need to know information and interaction routines, and they need to keep building an image of the ongoing conversation in their minds. **Information routines** are frequently occurring information structures such as stories, descriptions or comparisons. **Interaction routines** are typical turn structures that speakers know to belong to different types of situations such as service encounters, telephone conversations or lessons. The skills that learners need to use this knowledge are message planning skills, where the underlying knowledge of routines enables learners to predict what might happen and pre-plan their contributions, and interaction management skills, which Bygate divides into content-focused agenda management and interaction-focused turn-taking.

At the *selection* stage, learners use their knowledge of lexis, phrases and grammar to choose how to say what they want to say. The skills related to this, according to Bygate, have to do with negotiation of meaning. **Explicitness skills** enable learners to choose their expressions in the light of what they estimate the hearer to know, while **procedural skills** help them make sure that understanding takes place, for example through emphasis, repetition, or requests for clarification, etc. Together, the planning and selection activities can be called interactional skills, as they have to do with how speakers relate to others in conversation.

Figure 5.2 A summary of oral skills (Bygate, 1987: 50)

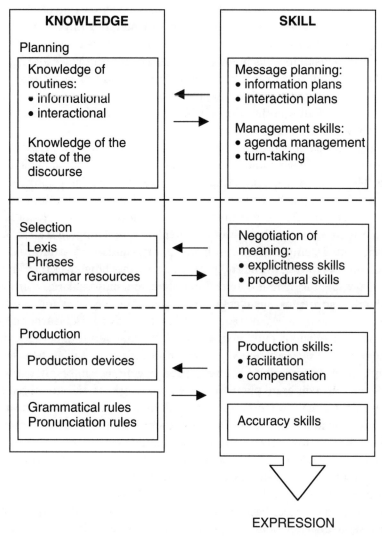

Production activities are closely related to the time-bound nature of speaking. The knowledge required here is articulation and the speaker's knowledge of grammatical and pronunciation rules. The related skills are facilitation and compensation. Speakers can **facilitate** their speech production by simplifying structure, or by using ellipsis, formulaic expressions, and fillers and hesitation devices. Learners might find it useful to get feedback on this aspect of their speech because it might help them see how they can make speaking easier for themselves. **Compensation skills**, in turn, are very similar to facilitation, but they are used by speakers when something has gone wrong in their talk, or when they think that something might do unless they do something to get over the possible difficulties. Compensation skills involve the easy use of formulaic expressions, self-correction, rephrasing, repetition via expansion or reduction, and hesitation. These expressions make speakers sound fluent even if, inside their minds, they feel that the speaking situation was quite demanding and they had to work a lot to do well in it.

Bygate considers the processing and reciprocity conditions of speaking to be the same for first and second language speakers, but he recognises that learners need special strategies to compensate for gaps in their knowledge and skills. Following Faerch and Kasper (1983), he divides learner communication strategies into achievement and reduction. When learners use **achievement strategies**, they compensate for language gaps by improvising a substitute, for example by paraphrasing, guessing, borrowing words and phrases from other languages they know, or engaging the listener in collaborative meaning-making. Through **reduction strategies**, speakers change what they originally intended to say according to their language resources. Strategies make learner communication efficient, and traces of them in learner performances provide evidence that they are actively engaged in meaning-making. However, similarly to Bachman and Palmer (1996), Bygate recognises that strategies work on a different plane from the knowledge and skills required for speaking. Hence, strategies were not included in Figure 5.2, which summarises Bygate's view of speaking. Feedback on strategy use might nevertheless be useful, especially in learning-related assessment.

In fact, Bygate's approach to speaking as a whole is probably particularly useful for learning-related assessment of speaking. The organisation into planning, selection and production skills, or interaction and production skills, provides a clear basis for organising learning activities and choosing tasks to develop them. Assessment tasks, then, can also be selected on this basis, so that the results can be used to support further learning.

One example of using Bygate's model in this way is provided in Hasselgren (1998). She suggests that by observing examinees' use of fluency-enhancing smallwords, they can be offered concrete feedback about the strengths and weaknesses of their speaking skills. Playing for time with expressions such as *well, sort of* and *you know* is a helpful planning skill, while acknowledging the interlocutor with expressions such as *you know, you see* and *really* helps construct a coherent social conversation. Expressions such as *well, anyway* and *right* can support the information structure of a conversation. Facilitation and compensation skills can be evidenced for example through expressions such as *You mean...?,* *a kind of* and *what*, while vague expressions signalling lack of total commitment such as *kind of, loads of* and *I think* help in the negotiation of meaning by allowing room for interpretation (Hasselgren, 1998: 169).

Applying the models in test design

The first step in any test development project is to analyse the assessment needs of the situation where the test is being developed. At the next stage, when the developers define the construct to be assessed, theoretical models can be helpful. They can offer wordings and provide criteria for evaluating the comprehensiveness of the test. In this final section of the chapter, I will discuss some examples of using models for this.

Models as theoretical anchors

Speaking assessments are normally developed for 'applied' purposes such as providing feedback for further learning, giving course grades, or selecting people for training or employment, rather than for studying the validity of theoretical models. Thus, individual speaking assessments are rarely intended to implement all aspects of a theoretical model. However, by using a model as a theoretical anchor for describing which features of speaking are relevant for the practical purpose for which the test is being used, the developers can describe the nature of their assessment to people who have not been involved in the development.

Moreover, applied purposes are often truly applied in the sense that one theoretical perspective does not suffice to explain its concrete features. An eclectic approach to relating tests to models thus comes naturally to many assessment developers. The multiple perspectives provided for example by combining Bachman and Palmer's componential view with Bygate's procedural view of speaking make it possible for the developers to talk about the assessment to different audiences, for example colleagues and examinees.

One example of using a model as a theoretical anchor for a test is the Australian test for immigrating teachers who do not come from an English-speaking background. The test is called the English Language

Skills Assessment (ELSA) and it assesses immigrant teachers' ability to deal with school communication requirements in all four skills (McDowell, 1995). The developers chose to start from Bachman's (1990) Communicative Language Ability and formulate the definitions of the skills to be tested in terms of the grammatical, textual, illocutionary and pragmatic features of teachers' language use in schools. The oral subtest emphasised pragmatic competence. To facilitate this, the decision was made to assess the candidates in pairs 'to provide a forum for some kind of interactive communication and thus to judge a candidate's control of register, his or her sense of appropriacy and sensitivity to other speakers' (McDowell, 1995: 21). The test involves a role-play between examinees and a group discussion between the two examinees, the interlocutor and the assessor. The performances are rated in four areas: interactive communication, intelligibility, appropriacy and accuracy. These criteria focus on the properties of the candidates' use of language, and only bear an indirect relationship to the CLA model.

A related example is the development of the Australian English as a Second Language (ESL) bandscales for describing ESL learners' language learning in the Australian primary and secondary school system (McKay, 1995). The versions of the CLA model that were used in this project were the 1990 Bachman version and a working version of the 1996 model by Bachman and Palmer. The practical context of the assessment and the more abstract contextual framework of Australian education policy also had a significant effect on the project. McKay (1995: 44) explicitly states that the project used a 'weak' interpretation of the Bachman and Palmer (1996) model, using it as a general guide rather than an absolute rule. The developers wrote frameworks for assessment activities, which specified expectations of background knowledge specific to the teaching context, identified significant assessment activities that corresponded to the real-life circumstances of teachers, stated guidelines for implementing the assessment, and suggested main aspects of language use to be assessed (McKay, 1995: 46–47). However, both the task features and the assessment criteria were driven by the needs of schools and pupils rather than the CLA model.

Models as sources of scoring categories

One concrete application of models in test development is using them to inform the organisation and wording of scoring criteria. This has been done for example with the Test of Spoken English (TSE) (ETS, 2001), as discussed in Chapter 4. The overall rating criterion is communicative effectiveness, while the four analytic criteria are functional, sociolinguistic, discourse, and linguistic competence (Douglas and Smith, 1997). Thus, they follow the four main areas of Bachman's (1990) CLA. However, the definition of functional competence has been modified slightly so that it refers to the examinees' fulfilment of the speech act functions tested in the TSE and not Halliday's broader framework of functions of language use. This is because communicative functions in the speech act sense are a central organising principle in the TSE and, broadly speaking, they can be considered to belong to the area of functional competence or knowledge in the CLA. Thus, the scoring method of the TSE forges a link between the theoretical framework, task design, and scoring procedures. The scales were discussed in Chapter 4.

Test-based model creation

Most test developers relate their test to existing theoretical models, but it is also possible to create a test-specific theoretical model, especially if the test development project is large enough to allow the use of a sizeable group of experts. This has been done in the case of developing TOEFL 2000, the next generation of the Test of English as a Foreign Language (see the TOEFL website by ETS at www.toefl.org). The published reports of this ongoing project currently cover the initial stages of background investigations and model and framework development but not yet any analyses of test prototypes. The test will assess reading, writing, listening and speaking, both in isolation and in various combinations, but the underlying theoretical model is the same for all parts of the assessment.

The TOEFL 2000 model was created by the TOEFL Committee of Examiners, a test development co-ordination body at ETS. After its creators, the model has been called the COE Model (Chapelle, Grabe and Berns, 1997). It defines communicative language use in academic contexts. The two main parts of the model are 'internal operations' and 'context'. According to Chapelle *et al.* (1997: 2), the model represents a summary of 'existing research and current assumptions by researchers in cognitive psychology, applied linguistics, and language testing' with particularly strong influences from Hymes (1971), Canale and Swain (1980), and Bachman (1990). The model is reproduced in Figure 5.3.

Figure 5.3 The COE working model of communicative language use in an academic context (Chapelle *et al.*, 1997: 5)

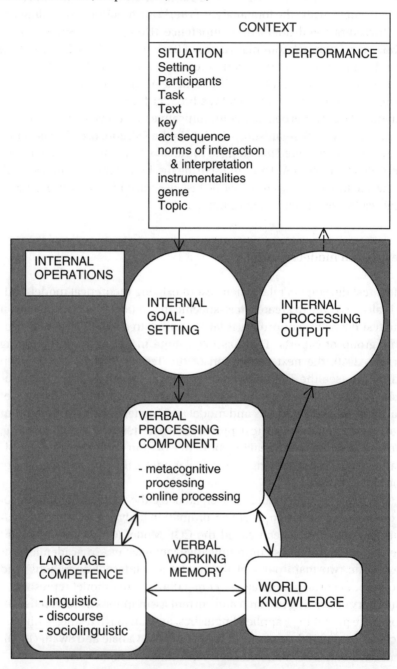

In the COE model, the context consists of two interacting factors: situation and performance. The situation in the case of TOEFL 2000 is academic, for example a lecture or an office appointment, and the model outlines those features of it that are expected to influence academic language use, namely:

- setting (i.e. physical location);
- participants (i.e. the individuals and their roles);
- task (i.e. a piece of work or an activity with a specified goal);
- text (i.e. type of language used to complete a task), and;
- topic (i.e. the content information that is being addressed).

Performance is seen as the language user's contribution to the context. This comprises the language and action of the language user in the situation. The authors do not claim that these variables are new, but rather they have chosen to build a new model out of existing theoretical knowledge that applies to their particular setting: academic communication in English.

The language user's abilities are considered as interrelated internal operations, which are represented by a range of processing components in the grey box in Figure 5.3. The process begins with internal goal setting, which is motivated by the individual's perceptions of and responses to 'context'. The key internal operations happen in verbal working memory, which houses the interactions of a verbal processing component, language competence, discourse and sociolinguistic knowledge, and world knowledge. The result of this interactive processing is internal processing output, which is the language user's representation of the situation or activity 'so far' and which can lead to overt performance in terms of words and actions (Chapelle *et al.*, 1997: 10–17).

These components are considered to interact in any language-use situation, and the organising principle for their interaction is the situational context rather than the skills of listening, speaking, reading or writing. Accordingly, 'situation' was selected as the basic unit of context that test developers set out to define. If the model is taken seriously, this proposal means that the test should test integrated skills in situation-based tasks or test sections. However, the developers state that they also consider the traditional skills division useful, and therefore they intend to test skills both individually and in integration (Jamieson *et al.*, 2000).

The COE model identifies situational and internal components in communicative competence, but these are not enough to define the construct assessed in TOEFL 2000. Since the model explicitly sees communication as an interaction between an individual and the context, it leads the developers of TOEFL 2000 to examine the nature of North American academic contexts. The model guides them to identify key situations and hypothesise the abilities required by these in terms of goal setting, language processing, and linguistic, sociolinguistic and discourse competence. They should then construct relevant task formats and develop a scoring rubric for these (Chapelle *et al.*, 1997: 21–25). Whether this means that goal setting, language processing, and linguistic, sociolinguistic and discourse competence should then figure in the scoring and score reporting mechanisms is not specified by the COE model.

In other words, the way in which the COE model is used in TOEFL 2000 development does not differ very much in kind, though possibly more so in depth, from the practices of anchoring tests to generic models as discussed earlier in this chapter. The contribution of the COE model to theory development in language testing is its explicit connection of individually oriented processing approaches and more socially oriented context-based approaches to communicative language use, even if the main focus is still on the individual language user. Its contribution to practical test development in TOEFL 2000 is advice on the implementation of this link in actual test development work.

Conclusion

In this chapter, I have reviewed a range of models of communicative language ability and speaking that assessment developers can use to structure their work. Depending on the needs in the context where the assessment is being developed, they can use a single model or a combination of several different ones. However, the examples from practical assessment contexts showed that theoretical models only provide organisation for assessment development at a fairly abstract level. The rules that guide the construction of the test, including the definition of the construct and the detailed guidelines for tasks and rating criteria, need to be very concretely tied to the testing situation. This is the topic of the next chapter.

CHAPTER SIX

Developing test specifications

It is useful to begin the development of a test by writing test specifications, and this is what this chapter will discuss. The first part gives an overview of test specifications, their purpose and their contents. The second part presents three examples of specifications: one for a stand-alone speaking test in an EFL classroom, one for a university entrance examination, and one for a proficiency test for adults. The purposes of the tests are different (achievement, selection, certification), and so are the examinee populations. Nevertheless, the structure of the specifications is fairly similar.

Specifications: What? and why?

Anyone who develops a speaking assessment will have ideas about what kind of speaking it will focus on, how the assessment will be done, and what the rating criteria will be. The written version of these ideas is called the **test specifications,** or specs for short. The specifications contain the developers' definition of the construct(s) assessed in the test, and detailed definitions of the tasks and rating criteria to guide the development of comparable tasks and the delivery of fair ratings. The specifications record the rationale for why the assessment focuses on certain constructs, and how the tasks and criteria operationalise them.

There are several frameworks in language testing literature that explain the structure and the purpose of test specifications (e.g. Lynch and Davidson, 1994; Alderson *et al.*, 1995; Bachman and Palmer, 1996).

The recommendations that the different frameworks give for the contents of test specifications are almost identical. The most detailed list of contents is found in Alderson *et al.* (1995: 11–20, 38), according to whom the specifications should define:

- the test's purpose;
- description of the examinees;
- test level;
- definition of construct (theoretical framework for the test);
- description of suitable language course or textbook;
- number of sections/papers;
- time for each section/paper;
- weighting for each section/paper;
- target language situation;
- text-types;
- text length;
- language skills to be tested;
- language elements to be tested;
- test tasks;
- test methods;
- rubrics;
- criteria for marking;
- descriptions of typical performance at each level;
- description of what candidates at each level can do in the real world;
- sample papers;
- samples of students' performance on task.

The authors also say, however, that different versions of the specifications should be tailored for the needs of different readerships, and that the most detailed specifications will only be needed by the test developers and validators.

Lynch and Davidson (1994) and Alderson *et al.* (1995) propose that all the contents listed above should be compiled in one document: the test specifications. Bachman and Palmer (1996) suggest dividing largely the same contents into two different documents: the design statement, which contains the background definitions for the test, and the test blueprint, which specifies the structure of the test and also contains the test task specifications. These define, for each task: its purpose, constructs, setting, time allotment, instructions, and the linguistic features involved. Another approach, the one presented in this book, sees specifications as a single document, but a modular one. The contents are the same as in the other models of specifications, but conceptually they are grouped into three modules: construct specifications, assessment specifications and task specifications. The advantage is that each module focuses on one conceptual part of test development. Whichever model of specifications the developers of a particular test decide to follow, the main point is that specifications constitute a record of the underlying principles of the test. They guide the development of the test and provide information for score use and validation.

Detailed specifications for individual tests or assessments are not published very often. This does not mean that they are not written, however. Big testing organisations need them, because they have several people working on each part of the development and they need to make sure that they all work towards the same goals. In one-teacher classroom assessments, specifications are not needed for the same reason, but they are useful because they make test development more focused and help connect assessment with teaching and learning. For this purpose, in fact, it is worth writing specifications even afterwards, after a teacher has developed and maybe even used a test.

The most important practical advantage of writing specifications is that they will help the developers create a coherent system whose parts fit together. If the developers have never written speaking tests before, writing specifications together with the first versions of the tasks and scales will help them avoid some problems with test use. For example, they can avoid only gathering one kind of speaking performance, or finding, after the test has been administered, that the rating criteria do not work well with the performances. If the developers have tested speaking before but have not written specifications for the tests they have used, writing these at a later stage will help them revise the test for future administrations, and use their practical experience systematically when developing new assessments in the future.

A second group of advantages for writing specifications has to do with the developers' awareness of the theoretical underpinnings of their assessment. Beginning an assessment development project by writing specifications will help the developers focus conscious attention from the start on the concept of speaking behind the assessment. Writing specifications at a later stage will help them make the theory of speaking that is implicit in the assessment more explicit and observable. In both cases, the developers will be making concrete connections between the theory and practice of oral assessment in their own context, through their own data. This helps them participate in practical and theoretical discussions on assessing speaking with insights based on a set of data, which means that they know how some ideas work in practice and what concerns arise when they are applied.

Once developers have written specifications for their own test or assessment, they will find it easier to talk informatively about it with colleagues, be they teachers or testing specialists. In this way, specifications assist collaboration between various people who are interested in assessing speaking. Writing specifications for one's own test will also make the writers more informed readers of other people's specifications. They will be better able to ask relevant questions, both of other people's specifications and of the current version of their own.

Specifications are always best considered a working document, constantly evolving through the use of the assessment. They can also be a base for a historical record of how the assessment has evolved and which lessons have led to the various developments. The document would also provide valuable information for test development theory. Data on the causes and consequences of change are one potential basis for insights into the forces at work behind test development and use, an area that is not well documented in the existing language testing literature.

Modular specifications

Modular specifications typically consist of three of four parts. The starting point is the construct module, which defines the skills to be assessed. This is closely connected to the task and assessment specifications. The optional part is the history module. The structure of modular specifications is shown schematically in Figure 6.1.

The idea in the **construct specifications** is to define the relationship between the abstract definition of the skills assessed and the concrete implementation of them in the tasks and criteria. In this way, construct specifications define the construct *in context*. They describe the assessment situation (the purpose of the test and its nature as a speaking situation), give an overview of the tasks and the rating criteria, and then describe the speaking skills to be assessed in a clear and concrete way.

Figure 6.1 Modular specifications

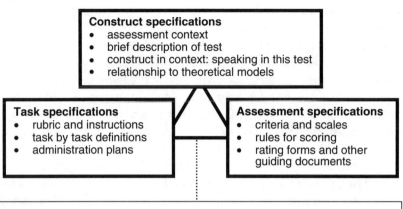

Construct specifications
- assessment context
- brief description of test
- construct in context: speaking in this test
- relationship to theoretical models

Task specifications
- rubric and instructions
- task by task definitions
- administration plans

Assessment specifications
- criteria and scales
- rules for scoring
- rating forms and other guiding documents

History file
- index of changes, organised by time
  WHEN was the change made? WHAT was changed? WHY was it changed?
- actual documents related to the change, the more clearly organised the better

Relating this description to existing models of speaking or other relevant reference frameworks, as discussed in the previous chapter, will make the definition more structured. The result is a 'grounded' summary definition of speaking, and once it has been written it guides everything in the assessment development process. The task and assessment specifications as well as all the tasks and criteria must cohere with it. It is also an important record for validation.

The **task specifications** begin with a definition of the tasks that the assessment consists of and a specification of the information and instructions about the test that will be given to test takers. These were outlined in Chapter 3. The task specifications also contain detailed definitions of each of the tasks, including item types and the skills to be assessed. In large testing systems, sample items are also commonly supplied in order to show what the specifications mean in practice. Finally, task specifications also include an evaluation of the resources required for administration and an outline of the actual administration process. This is especially important in interactive tests of speaking, where administration is individual. To be fair to all examinees, the administration procedures should be similar for them all.

The **assessment specifications** define the rating criteria and specify the way in which they are to be used during the rating process. Rating criteria were discussed in Chapter 4. In large tests, assessment design also includes procedures for rater training and monitoring of the rating process; these will be discussed in Chapter 8. In small-scale tests, a simple assessment plan is enough. It is important that the criteria are developed in coherence with the construct and task specifications. This is an iterative process, as the criteria are usually refined and re-worded several times while a test is being developed. It may be useful to keep copies of successive versions of the criteria and to record the development in a history file. It is easy to forget rationales for changes after a few versions, and keeping actual copies with development dates on them may save time and energy when debating further developments.

The **history file** is a record of changes in the assessment procedure. This is not a standard part of test specifications as they are discussed in testing textbooks and, in practice, the historical records of test development projects often consist of a jumbled assortment of draft tasks, criteria, and specification definitions from different stages of development. With a simple index sheet, however, this can be turned into a history file for the test. The index sheet only needs to include three columns labelled WHEN (a change was made), WHAT (was changed) and WHY. Then, if the need arises to make a more extended account of the development, it will help organise the documents in the file. Analysing the changes and their effects is useful for the test developers in a similar sense as learning diaries are useful for language learners. It encourages self-monitoring and qualitative development. In whichever form, the history file provides a useful resource when presenting the assessment project to outsiders and/or when sharing the expertise that the developers have accumulated in the course of their work.

In the rest of this chapter, I will discuss the writing of the first module of the specifications, the construct module. I will give three examples and describe the process through which the developers produced their definitions. This phase of specification-writing provides material for task and assessment specifications as well, but since these are large topics in themselves I will discuss them separately in Chapters 7 and 8. Here, I will start with an outline of the specification-writing process and continue with the examples.

Writing construct specifications

The aim in writing construct specifications is to produce a detailed, contextualised definition of the construct. The following steps give supporting questions for writing it. These can be useful, especially for someone who is writing specifications for the first time. I recommend starting the writing process from the concrete details of the context and working towards a more abstract formulation of the definition, because in this way the connections between the definition and the actual assessment procedure become firmer.

Describing the assessment context

This step involves general, introductory questions about the assessment. By answering these, the developers explain the context of their assessment to outsiders and, possibly, clarify it for themselves.

- What is the purpose of this assessment (evaluating overall proficiency, evaluating students' achievement of course goals, diagnosing strengths and weaknesses in speaking, etc.)?
- In what kind of an institutional context will it be arranged?
- Who are the examinees?
- What is their second language learning background?
- Who is the tester?
- What kind of a relationship is there between the tester and the examinees?
- Who see the scores, and how do they use them?

Characterising the assessment procedures

This step involves general questions about the assessment procedure itself. In most assessment contexts, there will be broad expectations, perhaps even requirements, for what the procedures should be like. There will also be practical limitations to what is possible in terms of available resources. The test has to be developed within these parameters.

- How should the test be administered?
- How long should the test be for an individual examinee?
- How often will it be organised?
- What kinds of tasks will the test include?
- When and how will the performances be assessed?

Towards describing the construct

This step in writing the construct definition focuses the developers' attention on learner language to help describe the skills to be assessed. The answers are also useful for creating and refining rating criteria for the test.

- What is 'speaking' for these learners, in terms of this test/assessment procedure?
- What kinds of tasks should be used in order to get at this kind of speaking?
- How would you characterise a good performance on these tasks?
- How would you characterise a poor performance on these tasks?
- What is an average performance like on these tasks?
- Is it useful for this assessment to consider speaking as consisting of sub-skills? If so, what?
- What other skills does the test-taking require in addition to language?

Relating the construct description to models and frameworks

As a result of the previous step, the developers have a working draft of their construct definition that is based on their plans for rating criteria and tasks. Next, they should use these ideas to point them in the direction of theoretical models and other frameworks that are relevant, and use these to evaluate and refine the definition.

- Which models or approaches to defining language ability and speaking are relevant for this test?
- Which aspects of these models are relevant for this particular test? How are they covered in the tasks and rating procedures?
- Which aspects of the models are not so relevant? Why?

The choice of the particular models that will be used is largely guided by the range of models the developers are familiar with, although they can also consult colleagues or textbooks. With the chosen models, it is important to consider what aspects of speaking are involved in this particular assessment procedure, but it is equally important to say which aspects are *not* covered in it. Both help define what is assessed. It is impossible to evaluate well all aspects of speaking with any single test, whatever it is like, so all-encompassing construct definitions do not sit easily with the group of concrete tasks to be used. It should be reasonably easy, on the other hand, to relate a well-defined test-based construct to the tasks and criteria.

Summarising the construct definition

The previous steps should have given the developers a resource of words with which to express their test-related ideas, as well as a comfortable sense that they know how to say what they are doing. In this last step of the construct definition process, the developers should review their answers to the above questions and summarise them in a clearly worded statement about what will be assessed and how. Some prompts to assist this work are:

- In a few simple phrases, what does this assessment procedure aim to assess?
- Which aspects, skills or abilities related to speaking are *not* covered in these particular procedures?
- For each key phrase describing what will be assessed, describe how that idea is reflected in examinee performances.

In addition to the texts written as products of the groups of questions above, the examples in the rest of the chapter include two further sections of text. At the beginning, there is some background information for the examples. At the end of each example, I will include a brief discussion of the construct definition.

The examples below begin with the final product, the construct definition. This is followed by a summary of the steps described above. In addition, I will give some background information on the specification-writing context and a brief discussion of the construct definition.

Example 1: An end-of-course classroom test

Construct definition
The aim of this test is to assess the examinees' ability to express their ideas in English, take their interlocutor's contributions into account and make use of them in the discussion, and collaborate in the creation of interaction. Social appropriateness is not assessed explicitly.

Ability to express own ideas is reflected in:

- intelligible pronunciation;
- knowledge of relevant vocabulary;
- ability to react in reasonable time and in relevant, meaningful chunks;
- sufficiently accurate knowledge of grammar.

Ability to take into account and make use of the interlocutor's turns and ability to collaborate in the creation of interaction are reflected in:

- signalling of known and new themes through phrasing, grammar and stress;
- repetition and reformulation of words and phrases from previous turns;
- relevance of turn content in light of previous turn and discourse history;
- willingness to talk, willingness and ability to elaborate.

Background to Example 1

Example 1 comes from a classroom testing context where one teacher tests a class of students. She has been arranging speaking tests for her graduating classes once a year for four years. At the beginning, her test development was a continuation of her teaching work, and she felt that little else besides tasks and rating criteria were needed. She knew a variety of test formats she wanted to try out; she had developed the syllabus on which the test was based; and she was the sole test writer, administrator and assessor, so no agreements between testers had to be made. In the course of the four years, she tried out various speaking tests on three different age groups. She gained experience in the way that different task types worked and in the kinds of problems that come up in administering classroom tests of speaking. She also became aware of the need to structure her test development to a greater degree so that she could develop her own skills and the quality of her tests. To get started, she used the process described above. The texts below are my summarised translations of her responses to the sets of questions outlined above, accepted as accurate by the teacher.

The assessment context

This test is given to students in the last term of their final year of comprehensive school. The students are 15–16 years old, and they have been learning English as a foreign language for seven years. They have had an average of two weekly lessons each year. Outside school, most students come into daily contact with English through pop music, imported TV programmes and films, but English is not an official language in the country, and the students rarely use English for real-life purposes outside the classroom.

The test scores are used by both the learners and the teacher. The learners use them as feedback on their speaking skills, and the teacher to assess the stage of development of the learners as well as to evaluate the success of her syllabus. Perhaps most importantly for all concerned, however, the results also count towards the grade for English that the students get in their school-leaving certificate. The scores cannot be the sole reason for lowering any student's final grade, but they can improve it. According to the teacher, this has in fact happened with some students whose written skills were weak.

Brief description of the test

The test is a formal complement to continuous assessment of speaking skills, and is given in the spring of the final year. It is given by the English teacher, who has been teaching these students for three years. The test is a paired interview led by the teacher/interlocutor, and it takes place in a separate classroom, mostly during normal English lessons. The teacher is responsible for both the class and the test situation. She can make it work because the students are used to working autonomously. After starting the lesson with the whole class, the teacher can administer two tests before coming back to class to finish the lesson. As there are around twenty students in a class each year, it will take five lessons, with possibly a few extra-curricular test sessions, to conduct a full round of tests.

For the pairs of examinees, the test is approximately 15 minutes long and contains four tasks: a warm-up, a description plus discussion task between the two students, a role-play, and a wind-down. The teacher's interaction outline for this test was discussed in Chapter 3. The task types will be discussed in Chapter 7.

The test situation is video-taped and the teacher rates the performances afterwards from the tape. The assessment is given as an analytic profile, and the features assessed are intelligibility of pronunciation, vocabulary, grammar and fluency. Scores for each of the features are reported on a five-point scale, which will be discussed in Chapter 8.

Descriptive definition of the construct

This is a test of spoken interaction, where the foreign language, here English, is a means of communication rather than an end in itself. The interaction deals with real-world issues, which the participants have learned about in daily life or in their other subjects. The students' speaking skills are reflected in the degree to which they can express their ideas in English, take into account and make use of their interlocutor's contributions to the discussion, and collaborate in the creation of interaction.

The test tasks must consist of real-time interaction. The dialogues can be semi-structured or loosely structured; above all, they must give the opportunity for the examinees to express their ideas and react to the interlocutor's turns. Both long and short turns should be elicited, and the learners should get opportunities to speak in different contexts. The students should show their willingness and ability to talk, but if some students have trouble with this it should be possible for the teacher to provide support so that at least some performance can be recorded from all participants.

A good performance would reflect the examinees' ability to express themselves comprehensibly in terms of intelligible pronunciation, relevant vocabulary and sufficiently accurate grammar, as well as in terms of information structuring and relevance of content. The performance would show evidence that the student is able to express him – or herself concisely but also to elaborate when necessary. Good performances would also show that the examinees understand the interlocutor's turns and know how to fit their own turns to these to create a coherent discussion. Excellent performances would show extensive lexical and phrasal knowledge and a natural rate of speech, with intonation contours contributing to the effectiveness of the communication. There would be little or no evidence of incomprehension of the interlocutor's turns, and no evidence of incoherence beyond what is normal for spoken texts in the real world.

At its worst, a bad performance would show little evidence of language ability at all. The examinee would not utter many words and would show few signs of having comprehended the interlocutor's turns. A typical bad performance would show evidence of some control over lexical items and some comprehension of the interlocutor's turns through relevant phrases or beginnings of replies, but the interaction would be characterised by incoherence due to long pauses or the examinee's inability to continue the discussion or complete a turn with the kind of content he or she might wish to express. Pronunciation may require a lot of attention, but it may also be relatively clear and thus easily the best feature of a weak examinee's performance.

Average performances on the test would yield a discussion that is coherent most of the time but now and then a speaker would produce an incoherent turn, or the tie between the speaker's and the previous speaker's turns would be awkward. Lexical approximation and/or clear grammatical errors would be apparent all through the examinee's talk, though few or no complete breakdowns in communication would occur. Pronunciation, particularly concerning rhythm and stress, might require some getting used to.

A very important subskill in this test is knowledge of words and phrases. Language use always involves words and phrases, of course, but because this is a speaking test the examinees have to be able to retrieve the words and phrases for use in a reasonable time as they become relevant in the test discourse. This constitutes a part of what in this test is called fluency. However, this is not the whole of the meaning of fluency in this test, the other parts having to do with the ability to produce comprehensible chunks of meaning and the ability to make contributions relevant to the discussion. The definition of fluency deserves more attention in future developments of the test, but in spite of its present state of vagueness it cannot be left out of consideration because it is a salient aspect of examinee speech to the teacher, both when it is well controlled and when it is not.

The performances on the test vary in terms of their grammatical accuracy. Some of them show virtually no consistently mastered structures; others include only simple structures with, for example, the use of only one tense. Some performances include a range of structures but they are full of errors, while others show an increasingly wide range of structures produced spontaneously and used correctly. Grammatical accuracy is an important learning objective in the curriculum, and thus it is also included as an assessment criterion in the test.

Intelligibility of pronunciation is a significant subskill in this test, both because it affects overall comprehensibility and because it is an aspect of speech that the examinees can improve on once they get feedback on their skills.

In addition to language-related abilities, the test requires an interactional orientation, confidence and willingness to talk. These have to do with personality and the examinees' communication skills in general.

The test also requires some creativity and ability to put new ideas into words on the spur of the moment. Moreover, the results are to some extent dependent on interpersonal compatibility between the pairs, which is why the examinees can choose their partners for the test themselves. As far as this test is concerned, there are few ways of excluding these additional factors from the assessment; the best means of dealing with this is awareness of potential problems during assessment.

Relationship to models of language ability

Given the focus on communication and language skills, the models that are relevant as construct frameworks for this test are Bachman and Palmer's (1996) CLA and Bygate's speaking model. With respect to the CLA, the test covers grammatical knowledge and some aspects of textual, functional and sociolinguistic knowledge, although explicit testing of sociolinguistic knowledge is not included. Grammatical knowledge is apparent in the test performances in all the turns that an examinee makes, and it is assessed through three criteria: vocabulary, grammar and pronunciation. Textual knowledge is evidenced in the examinees' ability to structure their ideas and make their contributions relevant. This is mostly assessed as part of fluency and vocabulary, though grammar contributes to coherence as well. If there are some problems with coherence in a test performance, this would most likely affect the fluency and vocabulary scores.

Functional knowledge is assessed somewhat vicariously in this test, since there is little direct elicitation of functions. In the course of the test interaction, the examinees are expected to provide descriptions as well as interpretations, opinions, and reasons for them, but their ability to express these is assessed through vocabulary, grammar, pronunciation and fluency rather than through a separate, abstractly worded criterion related to language functions.

Sociolinguistic knowledge is involved in the examinees' performances as it is an aspect of any interaction, but it is not tested explicitly, for example by varying the degree of formality in different tasks. The students are expected to use a polite familiar register appropriate for (supervised) school interactions.

In terms of Bygate's model of speaking, the test requires that the examinees have both language knowledge and skill to use it. The three areas of knowledge that Bygate defines as relevant for speaking, i.e. grammar, pronunciation and vocabulary, should all be present in the performances, and all are assessed through separate criteria. The criteria do not only cover knowledge but also the skills to use it. Thus, successful achievement strategies in particular would improve the examinees' scores on vocabulary or grammar, and ability to negotiate meaning would be rewarded in vocabulary and fluency scores. Information planning is not in central focus in the test, since the preparation time is really only used for familiarisation rather than detailed planning or rehearsal. Agenda management is tested to some extent, as the test consists of paired interaction, which the students have to structure themselves. At the level of the test phases, however, the teacher is responsible for managing the progress of the test.

Discussion

The construct definition for this test is communicatively oriented. The central portions of the test are conducted between a pair of students, while the teacher opens and closes the test discussion and leads the pair from one stage of the test to the next. The relationship between the tasks and the construct definition is fairly harmonious. The kinds of language skills specified in the definition could conceivably come up in this type of structured interaction test.

In comparison, the relationship between the construct description and the envisioned rating criteria is more complex and possibly problematic. While the criteria are called pronunciation, vocabulary, grammar and fluency, the construct definition also takes up relevance of turn content and various features to do with collaboration in interaction. The teacher might consider revising the criteria in connection with further testing rounds. The feedback she gives to the students on their communication skills might provide suggestions for new criteria.

Example 2: A language test at university entrance

Construct definition
This test assesses the examinees' oral proficiency in English in academic contexts. The goal is to distinguish between those prospective students whose oral proficiency is sufficient for them to enter full-time study, those who need some tuition in spoken English to support their studies, and those

who require a large amount of tuition in oral interaction in English. The criterion is *ability to understand* and *make oneself understood* especially *in academic situations*:

Ability to understand is reflected in:

- relevance of content and form of the examinee's turns to the taped prompts;
- appropriate linking to the prompt even if the content of the response is somewhat divergent from standard responses.

Ability to make oneself understood is reflected in:

- clear pronunciation;
- recognisable and effective intonation patterns;
- sufficiently accurate knowledge of grammar;
- knowledge of vocabulary relevant for both academic and social contexts;
- ability to react in reasonable time and in relevant, meaningful chunks;

The context of academic English is implemented through;

- the setting of the tasks in academic contexts;
- the provision of task materials, which create shared context between examinees and raters in simulation of the shared knowledge of participants in non-test academic communication.

Background to Example 2

The test in this example is a university entrance examination – the Canadian Academic English Language Assessment, or CAEL Assessment for short (CAEL, 2002). Its development began when the university community expressed a need to find an alternative to the TOEFL (Test of English as a Foreign Language) (Educational Testing Service, 2002). The development was a collaborative effort between English for Academic Purposes (EAP) teachers and academics in various faculties of the university. It was based on an analysis of the actual language performance requirements in first-year classes. The developers interviewed instructors and students, observed classes, and analysed tests, lab and essay assignments, and students' notes from all the faculties of one university. The results of the analysis were distilled into the test specifications and first drafts of tasks (Fox *et al.*, 1993).

In writing the specifications for all the test sections, speaking included, the developers followed Lynch and Davidson's (1994) iterative specification-writing model, which means that they made several cycles between specifications and task development and refined the definitions and tasks in the light of each other. In the discussion below, I discuss the information available from the existing specifications, which does not include a descriptive definition of the construct as in the other two examples in this chapter.

The assessment context

The purpose of the Oral Language Test, similarly to the whole CAEL Assessment, is (1) to identify the students who are able to meet the linguistic demands of full-time study, (2) to place students in EAP credit courses if additional linguistic support is needed at the beginning of their academic program, and (3) to identify students who require full-time English instruction in preparation for later studies. Each of the four skills is assessed separately in the CAEL Assessment, and the speaking score is used for decisions concerning the students' needs for oral skills courses.

The examinees are undergraduate and graduate students preparing to enter full-time study at an English-medium university. Thus, the examinees represent two fairly homogenous populations, and are typically 20–30 years old. While their future needs for language use are fairly uniform within each of the two groups, their language-learning backgrounds are highly varied. No one has English as their mother tongue, while some may have received all or part of their education in English. Some will have learned English as a foreign language, and may or may not have used English for real-life purposes outside the classroom.

The raters are teachers in the English language courses at the university and graduate students in the MA in Applied Linguistics program who are specialising in teaching English as a second or foreign language. When students sit the test at the end of their language course, their own teachers are not allowed to assess their performances.

The CAEL Assessment is administered as a three-stage process. In the first stage, the students register for the test and get information about its structure and contents. The next stage involves taking the OLT. Completion of this part entitles the examinees to take the rest of the test. The same process is followed whether the test is administered in Canada or abroad. In addition to registration, information about the structure of the OLT is available in leaflets, information materials and practice tests obtainable from www.carleton.ca/slals/cael.htm.

Task design

The OLT focuses on academic language use and contains five tasks: giving a short oral presentation about a topic that the participants get during registration, relaying information obtained from a lecture, relaying information obtained from a short written document, reading aloud a text for discussion in a tutorial, and arranging to make a group project by listening to other speakers' inputs and explaining about one's own initial ideas about a topic. It is approximately 25 minutes long, and it is taken either in a group session or on a self-access basis in a language laboratory – on one administration site, which does not have a language laboratory, the test is administered individually in a room with two tape recorders.

The task design was driven by the analysis of first-year students' communication needs that the developers conducted when CAEL was first developed, although within the constraints of the tape-based setting. They have to be able to ask and respond to questions, and present their views and analyses. The tasks are integrated in the sense that each of them requires the combination of at least reading, listening and speaking; a task-based construct definition was discussed in Chapter 3.

Rating design

The performances are rated analytically task by task. The presentation is rated on comprehensibility, the information-relaying tasks on factual accuracy and relevance of responses, the read-aloud on ease and comprehensibility, and the initial ideas for a presentation on fluency and meaningfulness. The criteria were selected after analysing examinee performances. Their joint aim is to evaluate the effectiveness of the examinees' communication in academically relevant tasks. In addition to task scores, the raters also give an overall impression mark on a scale from 10 to 30 with five-point intervals. The two scores are combined into a total score for the test. The rating procedure is discussed in more detail in Chapter 8.

The total score of communicative effectiveness in speaking is the main outcome of the OLT, and it is used for making decisions about the examinees. For students who are placed in English language programs, diagnostic information on the weakest aspects of their speaking skills can be made available. These are based on notes that the raters make on the tasks where the examinees give long responses. The most useful aspects for reporting have been found to be pronunciation, intonation, syntax, lexical choices and hesitation. The diagnostic system focuses on weaknesses rather than strengths, which may appear counter-productive. However, this serves the needs of the test context: the test does not certify proficiency as such, it helps identify students who need language support in order to cope with their studies. For this purpose, identification of weaknesses is more important than identification of strengths, as the results inform the teachers of the needs of their students and provide guidance for the students' learning.

Relationship to models of language ability

The CAEL is a thematic test, and its design rationale builds on activity theory (see e.g. Lantolf, 2000). Discussing the writing section of the test, Fox (2001) describes how the developers consider the examinees' writing on the test to be a dialogic interaction on two activity planes. On one level, the examinees interact with the tasks, which require them to integrate information from different parts of the test and engage in a dialogue between these and other texts that they have experienced in the past. On another, the writers are interacting with the raters, showing them how well they can do the expected task. Fox emphasises the importance of the two layers, and suggests that, if the tasks in a test are linked and well contextualised in order to offer the writers and readers some common ground to build on, their respective expectations of the appropriate properties of the texts will change. Both parties will understand that the texts need to be linked to the task material and evaluated in the light of how well this is done, which means that the test-taking plane and the evaluation plane of activity and interpretation become more closely aligned. This interpretive world is also fairly closely related to the writing activities that the examinees will meet outside the test.

Although Fox (2001) does not discuss speaking, it can be seen from the rationale discussed above that its development follows a similar logic. The topic in the OLT is the same as in the rest of the test, many of the tasks provide ample resource material, and the examinees are expected to engage with the social environment that the tasks create, for example by re-using phrases and structures from it and combining these with their existing knowledge in their test responses. Thus, although the examinee-speakers and the rater-listeners do not share the same space and time, the shared context in the task materials creates 'covert collaboration' between them (Fox, personal communication).

Discussion

The OLT construct definition is clearly influenced by the purpose and format of the test. It emphasises the sociocultural approach of Activity Theory, which underlies the thematic orientation of the test and the view that the context is there to provide a shared background for the key actors, i.e. the speakers and the raters. The definition is very closely knitted with the tasks and criteria, which was reflected in the discussion above. More detailed examples of the tasks and criteria will be included in Chapters 7 and 8.

Example 3: A general purpose proficiency test

Construct definition

The aim of this test is to assess the examinees' ability to interact effectively in the test language. They should be able to use language appropriately in a range of different situations. They should also be able to make a clear, coherent presentation on a familiar topic, and be able to discuss topics of general interest as well as their own work.

Ability to interact effectively is a superordinate descriptor in the construct definition. It consists of the following aspects of speaking.

Ability to use language appropriately to different situations. This is reflected in the ability to:

- vary the degree of formality of phrases, idioms and structures depending on the situation;
- use varying politeness conventions (greetings, forms of address, mitigation);
- appropriate use of at least two registers: formal and informal.

Clarity of presentation. This stems from ability to:

- organise information in an easily comprehensible order, both at the level of the text and at the level of individual utterances;
- use discourse markers, repetition, and stress to emphasise important points and make the text structure more salient to the listeners.

Ability to discuss general and work-related topics. This is reflected in the ability to:

- express opinions concisely as well as elaborate them by specifying, exemplifying, giving reasons;

- take the interlocutor's contribution into account and tie the content and format of one's own turn to this;
- use strategies to enhance the effectiveness of one's contribution, e.g. using gestures, loudness, and rhythm; employing introductory phrases and set responses; explicitly signalling reference and structure of own contribution.

Prerequisites of the above specified abilities are:

- good knowledge of the vocabulary and structures of the language, and ability to access the knowledge relatively fast;
- comprehensible pronunciation;
- ability to comprehend and react to the interlocutor's speech.

If an examinee falls below a minimum threshold in any of these aspects, fulfilling the requirements of the test tasks appropriately is in serious jeopardy. Precision of lexical choices, accuracy of grammatical structures, and sensitivity to context in phrasing signal the learner's progress through the skill levels covered by this test.

Background to Example 3

The test in this example is the Finnish National Certificates, a general purpose proficiency test for adult language learners. The examination system has three test levels and ten test languages. The focus here is on the speaking subtest of the advanced level test. All the test languages use the same specifications although there are minor differences in task types between the languages. This is possible because the task specifications contain alternatives that the language-specific teams can choose from, while the construct specifications and most of the assessment specifications are the same for all the tests.

The development of the advanced level speaking test started from specification writing, which was followed by the drafting and initial trialling of the draft tasks. However, both the specifications and the tasks have continued to evolve throughout the development and use of the test.

The assessment context

The advanced level test in the Finnish National Certificates (NC) is a general purpose proficiency test. The speaking subtest consists of two parts, one of which is tape-based and the other live. The test is taken by adults who want feedback on their level of proficiency in a language or who need a certificate of language skills for educational or employment purposes. The certificates are recognised by some educational institutions in Finland, as well as by some state offices, which reward employees for proficiency in foreign languages. Many employers recognise the certificate as one way of proving a job applicant's language skills.

The examinees come from a fairly homogeneous linguistic and cultural background, but the ways in which they have learned their language skills may vary greatly. Most will have received some formal language teaching as part of their general and/or vocational education, but some may also have lived or worked in a country where the test language is used as a means of daily communication. The age range of the examinees is from 17 to 80, with a mean of around 35 years. Some participants use the test language in their work, while others do not. They select their test level when they sign up for the examination on the basis of general descriptions of the tests in information brochures. If they have recently taken a language course, they may ask the instructor for help. The description for the advanced level advises that the test is suitable for adults whose language skills match challenging tasks such as representing their workplace in specialist matters, and who can adjust their language use according to the demands of different situations.

Brief description of the test

The tape-based part of the test includes 3–4 tasks, while the live part contains 2–3 tasks. Both parts are approximately 15 minutes long. The tape-based tasks include reacting in various simulated situations and giving a mini-presentation, while the face-to-face tasks involve a thematic discussion on societal issues. The live test begins with a discussion of the examinee's professional or educational background, but it also covers other topics for which the examinee has not been able to prepare in advance.

The tape-based test is recorded on audiotape and the live test on videotape. The performances are double rated afterwards from the tapes. Analytic assessments are given on pronunciation, language flow, vocabulary and grammar. In addition, there are two section-specific rating criteria: interaction skills for the live part and textual organisation for the last task of the tape-based test, the mini-presentation. The analytic scores are combined into an overall score for speaking, which is reported to the examinees in the certificate.

The raters are language teachers or assessment specialists who have successfully completed rater training. For all the examinees to be in an equal position, the rater cannot be the examinee's own teacher or personal acquaintance.

Descriptive definition of the construct

This test assesses the examinees' ability to interact effectively in the test language in a range of social contexts from highly formal to informal. It tests the examinees' ability to discuss professional matters and topics of general interest, and their ability to interact with others as well as their ability to make presentations. The examinees must express themselves clearly, accommodate their language use to the situation, and contribute to the creation of coherent spoken discourse. The monologic tasks also assess the examinees' ability to structure their presentation to assist comprehensibility. The test makes distinctions between three levels of advanced proficiency. Appropriateness of language to different situations and lexical range and precision are significant in making these distinctions.

To evaluate this broad definition of speaking, the tasks must be very versatile. It is important that both structured and open-ended tasks are included, and that the topics of the test include the examinee's profession as well as other topical matters not directly related to their work. Variation in levels of formality should be included, although simulation of intimate situations or formal high-pressure situations may be difficult.

An excellent performance on the test reflects the examinee's facility with language use. The meanings are coherent and easily comprehensible, the lexical range impressive, and there is no evidence of unintended deviance from the norms of spoken grammar relevant to the situations included in the tasks. The examinee uses collocations and idioms naturally and is able to play with words and phrases. There may be one or two phrases which appear slightly odd to a native speaker listener, but which are nevertheless fully comprehensible in context.

Performances that fall below the requirements of the advanced level test are spoken at a slower than normal speaking rate and the examinee's rhythm and intonation patterns may be difficult to get used to. In the live test, they clearly require interlocutor support to make the discussion flow, and in the tape-based part one or two prompts may be left unanswered. The examinees have obvious difficulties expressing the meanings they intend to make. A minimally acceptable performance shows ability to deal with all the tasks of the test at some level, possibly with some lexical or grammatical difficulties. In the live part, unclear meanings are clarified through negotiation, while in the tape-based part some of the examinee's contributions are fully comprehensible and relevant but others marginally comprehensible.

Average performances display ability to deal with all the tasks of the test adequately, though in the live test the examinees may find it difficult to extend some topics to higher levels of abstraction. They may sometimes require additional support or detailed probing from the interlocutor, while at other times they contribute to the creation of interaction with ease. Control of either grammar or vocabulary is typically strong, while the other is weaker, or control of vocabulary is uneven such that the examinees' contributions are clear and natural in some areas while there is a surprising degree of lexical approximation in others. Pronunciation is comprehensible though rarely effortless; typical problems involve rhythm and intonation, or alternatively a somewhat intrusive mispronunciation of a few individual sounds.

Relationship to models of language ability

Given the number of linguistic features that were mentioned in the paragraphs above, the most relevant model for the test is the CLA. All the parts of the model are covered in the test to some extent. Grammatical knowledge is reflected in all the turns that the examinees make, and it is operationalised in the rating criteria of pronunciation, vocabulary and grammar. Textual knowledge is reflected in the coherence of the test discourse within and between the turns, and in the structuring of long turns on both parts of the test. The criteria that reflect this are discourse skills and textual organisation. Functional knowledge is tested explicitly in the tape-based test and implicitly all through the test. However, there is no separate criterion for functional ability. It is assessed as part of a criterion called 'appropriacy and discourse skills', which also covers sociolinguistic ability. This is tested especially in the tape-based task of reacting in situations, where the formality of the different situations varies. In the live test, sociolinguistic ability is tested more implicitly because there is only one context of interaction and one interactant relationship.

Bachman and Palmer (1996) distinguish three components within strategic competence: goal-setting, assessment and planning. Within the limits set by the test tasks, the examinees are expected to set their goals, be able to assess what is needed and what they have language-wise, and how well they have done, as well as plan their contribution to the test discourse during preparation and performance. All of the aspects of strategic competence are thus included in the test construct, though only to the extent that this is possible in a test situation. Strategic competence is not evaluated directly, but it is highly likely that it influences the ratings.

The construct of speaking in the test is obliquely related to Bygate's (1987) processing and reciprocity conditions. It may well be possible to explain the difference between a proficient speaker's good performance and a weak examinee's difficulties with expressing themselves by differences in their ability to process the language in real time, but there is little in the test that could provide direct proof of this. The test contains both fully reciprocal discourse and simulated, more planned monologic discourse. Skills in negotiating meaning are rewarded, although negotiation skills are not tested explicitly. A reasonably large vocabulary, good control over syntactic structures, and comprehensible pronunciation are considered minimum requirements for acceptable performances, but as Bygate points out, these knowledge components are necessary but not sufficient resources for speaking. On the whole, the construct definition is cognitive rather than sociocultural in its tone and orientation.

Discussion

Unlike the two previous construct definitions, this one defines a lower bound for the skills measured in the test, below which a performance is considered a fail. This is because the test is not meant for the whole ability continuum but only for advanced learners. This requires clear definitions in the rating criteria.

Summary

In this chapter, I have looked at the process of writing construct specifications for assessments of speaking. The starting point was that specifications for speaking assessments define what kind of speaking will be assessed, how this will be done, and which aspects of the performances are going to be evaluated. I presented three groups of reasons why the developers of speaking tests should write specifications.

- Practical: writing specifications will help create a test system whose parts fit together.
- Theoretical: writing specifications will force the writers to consider the theoretical underpinnings of what they are doing.
- Educational: writing specifications will enable the writers to discuss oral assessment in a focused manner and make better use of other test developers' experiences.

I proposed a modular approach to specifications, minimally consisting of construct, task and assessment specifications. The modular structure divides the task of specification writing into focused chunks, which can be worked on in whichever order best suits the needs of the test and the test developers. The specifications could also include a history file, in which developments in the test are recorded on a time line. This is useful for recounting the evolution of the test, but also, and perhaps more importantly, as a source that enables the test developers to reflect on their own activities.

The writing of construct specifications was illustrated with three examples. These involved a five-step writing process, which produced concrete verbal descriptions of what each test was focused on. In Chapter 7 on tasks and Chapter 8 on rating procedures, I will discuss some of the tasks and criteria related to these specifications, as well as other examples of tasks and rating procedures.

CHAPTER SEVEN

Developing speaking tasks

In this chapter, I will begin with examples of speaking tasks in order to make the discussion concrete. As we saw in Chapter 6, test design starts from analysing the purpose of the test: what will the scores be used for, and what type of information do the score users need? This guides both the construct definition and the choice of tasks and criteria. If they define the purpose mainly in terms of language activities, they may decide to use different types of talk or language functions as the main design principle for the tasks. If they need information about the examinees' ability to deal with some specific speaking situations or some professional roles, they will use these as main categories in the task design. If they need information about aspects of the examinees' control of language, such as their pronunciation skills or their knowledge of certain grammar points, they may use highly structured tasks such as reading aloud or sentence completion, where they can control exactly what the examinees will say. All these types of tasks will be exemplified below.

Examples of speaking tasks

Description tasks

Here are two examples of description tasks.

Example 1: Interaction outline for a one-to-one interview
Describe to me the room or area where you work.

Example 2: Interaction outline for a pair task in an interview test

In this part of the test, I will give each of you a picture. Don't show the pictures to each other.

Hand over the pictures.

A   B

Please describe your pictures to each other and then talk about what is similar in your pictures and what is different. Student A, you begin.

Students A and B describe and discuss their pictures for about 2 minutes. If necessary, give them further prompts: describe the scenery, describe the town, what part of the world . . .

Approximately 2 minutes.

Thank you.

(Adapted from Heaton, 1991: 95)

Description tasks are very common in all kinds of speaking tests. They can be used in one-to-one interviews and with pairs, and they also suit tape-based testing. Example 1 is an extract from an interlocutor's script for a one-to-one interview, and it illustrates how concise description tasks can be, especially if the testers are really interested to know how well (comprehensibly, efficiently) the examinees can describe something they know. In response to the brief prompt, the examinee should give a much longer description. The object that the examinees are asked to describe can vary from one examinee to another, as the description task can arise from something that the examinees mention in their talk. All that the test developers need to decide is the limits for parallel tasks: is it physical descriptions of rooms or areas that they are after, or would person descriptions also suffice, or do all examinees perhaps need to provide both a spatial description and a person description? This design decision guides what the interlocutors will do. The criterion for judging the performances is whether the listener can picture what is being described, much as it would be in real life.

If the developers want to control the content of the descriptions, providing pictures, as in Example 2, is a very common alternative. This means that all the examinees will discuss the same topic area and use largely the same vocabulary in their performances. However, the communication in the task may become less genuine, since the testers *know* what the examinees are supposed to describe, and thus they have no real need to ask. This is why the examinees in Example 2 received two different pictures; it gives them a need to communicate. In designing description tasks, the developers need to consider carefully whether pictures will be needed. Creating them makes the development of description tasks more work-intensive, but especially in pair tasks they allow the developers to control the content of the task discourse and plan the size and length of the task.

Narrative tasks

Here is one example of a narrative task.

Example 3: Examinee's test booklet in a tape-based test

Now please look at the six pictures below. I'd like you to tell me the story that the pictures show, starting with picture number 1 and going through picture number 6. Please take one minute to look at the pictures and think about the story. Do not begin the story until you are told to do so.

Tell me the story that the pictures show. (60 seconds)

(ETS, 2002)

Here is another example of a narrative task.

Example 4: A face-to-face paired interaction test

Pupil A's booklet
Match day
You each have a set of pictures. Together they make a story about two teenagers going to a football match.

You have a picture from the beginning of the story, as well as pictures telling the second half of the story. Your friend's pictures tell the first half of the story.

Describe your first picture in as much detail as you can.

How do you think Steve and Ann feel?

Now **listen** to your partner telling the first half of the story.

Afterwards, you **tell** the rest of the story to your partner. Tell the story as Ann or Steve might tell it to a friend later.

How do you think Ann and Steve felt in pictures 6, 7 and 9?

Pupil B's booklet
Match day
You each have a set of pictures. Together they make a story about two teenagers going to a football match.

Your friend has a picture from the beginning of the story. You have the rest of the pictures telling the first half of the story, Your friend, then, has the pictures telling the second half.

Listen to your friend describing the first picture.

Now **tell** the first half of the story in as much detail as you can. Tell the story as Ann or Steve might tell it to a friend later.

How do you think Ann and Steve felt in pictures 3, 4 and 5?

Then **listen** to your partner telling the second half of the story.

Pupil A's pictures

Pupil B's pictures

(© Nasjonalt læremiddelsenter, Norway, 1996)

Narrative tasks are also frequently used in speaking tests. They show how well the examinees can recount a sequence of events, usually in one time frame, either present or past. Most often, the tasks are based on picture sequences, where the content of the pictures guides what will be said. The alternative would be to ask the examinees to tell something that happened to them. While stories about 'what happened to me' are very common in real life, they usually belong to social chatting, which is difficult to replicate in a test situation. They may work in educational settings where the participants know each other but, even then, the fit is not perfect. Personal stories often reveal embarrassing details that speakers would be shy to discuss in a test or, if not, they may be so uneventful that the speakers would consider them unworthy to tell. Hence, picture-based sequences are common but, as discussed in Chapter 3, the choice of good sequences is a difficult matter. They should generate enough talk and provide opportunities for the examinees to show what they know. In particular, they should make the examinees show their control of the essential features of narratives: setting the scene, identifying the characters and referring to them consistently, identifying the main events, and telling them in a coherent sequence. Whenever picture sequences are used, it is a good idea to try them out before actual use in the test to check that they work as intended.

In Example 3, the narrative is a monologue, and as the test is tape-based the examinees have to tell it in one long stretch without any feedback from a listener. Example 4, in contrast, is likely to create some interaction, even though one of the pupils is always the main speaker while the narrative is being constructed. The information gap means that there are in fact two tasks that the examinees are completing: they are making sense of the story for themselves, as they only know part of it to begin with, and telling it together. This requires some negotiation, as intended by the task developers. The task comes from a voluntary speaking test for 14–15-year-old Norwegian school pupils. The test is largely conducted between two examinees, which is why the written instructions are fairly detailed.

Instruction tasks

Here is an example of an instruction task.

Example 5: Interaction outline for a one-to-one interview

Do you have a favourite shop where you often buy groceries?

Even if not, get the examinee to identify some shop – for other products, if necessary.

Imagine that we are standing in front of your house. Tell me how to get to the shop from there.

Here is another example of an instruction task.

Example 6: A face-to-face paired interaction test

Pupil A's booklet
Feeding the puppy
You can't go home, and your puppy needs to be fed. Your friend says s/he will do it.

Tell your partner exactly what to **do**, what s/he'll **need** and where to **find** things. Follow the instructions below. Find what you need in the picture.

- Quick run in garden
- Food! (you need 1, 2 and 3)
- Drink! (you need 4)
- Walk! (you need 5)
- Home again! Wipe the puppy's feet and the floor (you need 6).
- More water?

Then check that s/he understands exactly what to do. **Ask her/him to go over** the main points of:

- what to do
- what s/he needs
- where to find things

(Help her/him to get it right.)

Pupil A's picture

FEEDING THE PUPPY

Pupil B's booklet
Feeding the puppy
You are going to look after your friend's puppy. S/he will give you exact instructions.

Listen carefully and **ask** if there's anything you don't understand.
At the end, check that you know what to do. **Try to tell your partner** these things:

- what you have to do
- what you need
- where to find things.

(© Nasjonalt læremiddelsenter, Norway, 1996)

The main purpose in giving directions and instructions is getting the message across and making sure that it has been understood. This tends to mean short exchanges between the speaker and the listener. The instruction-giver is the main speaker first, and the listener usually only agrees, unless there is a problem in understanding. If the listener has to remember the instructions, he or she usually repeats them at the end of the instruction-giving sequence. Thus, instruction giving suits live testing particularly well, but sometimes it is also used in tape-based tests, especially with maps. Interaction is obviously not included in that case, and the rating is focused on the accuracy and comprehensibility of the instructions given. In interactive tests, in contrast, the interaction between the speakers also tends to be included in what is evaluated. The task in Example 6 implements this carefully, with the instructions guiding both the instruction-giver and the listener to play their part.

Comparing and contrasting tasks

Here is an example of a comparison and contrast task.

Example 7: Interaction outline for a pair task in a paired interview

Protective clothing (compare, contrast and speculate)

Interlocutor   In this part of the test I'm going to give each of you the chance to talk for about a minute and to comment briefly after your partner has spoken.

First, you will each have the same set of photographs to look at. They show people wearing protective clothing.

Hand over the same set of photographs to each candidate.

Candidate A, it's your turn first. I'd like you to compare and contrast two or three of these photographs, saying what kind of clothing the people are wearing and why you think the protection might be necessary.

Don't forget, you have about one minute for this.

All right? So, Candidate A, would you start now, please?

Candidate A   *Approximately one minute.*

Interlocutor   Thank you. Now, Candidate B, can you tell us who you think is in the greater need of protection?

Candidate B   *Approximately 20 seconds.*

Interlocutor   Thank you.

Student pictures

(UCLES, 2001b)

Tasks that require comparing and contrasting are usually considered more demanding than description because they also require analysis and the discussion of similarities and differences. This requires the use of comparative forms and complex grammatical structures. The task demands also depend on the objects that are compared, however. In Example 7, the topic of protective clothing is somewhat abstract, and flexibly so depending on how each examinee interprets and the examiner's instructions of describing what the people are wearing and why this protection might be necessary. The combination of 'what' and 'why' increases the length of the talk that the pictures give rise to, and it also adds to the level of demand of the task. This makes effective use of the pictures and guides the examinees to treat the topic in some depth.

Comparison tasks are not always based on pictures; examinees can also be asked to compare concepts they are expected to know, such as the quality of life in urban and rural communities. In profession-specific assessments, they might be asked to compare the demands of two different kinds of work projects, for example, or the advantages and disadvantages of different treatments of a problem.

The task in Example 7 is completed by two examinees, and it has been designed to maintain the interest of them both. Examinee B first observes which two or three of the five pictures A picks, and then B is asked to compare the pictures from a different perspective. This is a special design consideration in paired testing. Moreover, in the Cambridge Certificate of Advanced English, which Example 7 comes from, this task is followed by another one of the same kind, where B is asked to take the first turn and A the shorter, second turn. This is done in the interest of fairness, as both examinees need to get the same opportunities to show their abilities. The Norwegian test in Example 6 followed the same practice, as do most other speaking tests.

Explaining and predicting tasks

Here is an example of an explanation and prediction task.

Example 8: Examinee's test booklet in a tape-based test

The following graph shows the number of workers in five different occupations in the United States in 1990 and the projected number for the year 2005. Take 15 seconds to look at the graph.

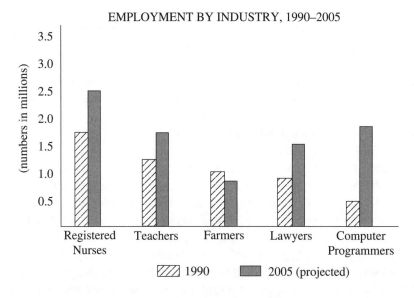

EMPLOYMENT BY INDUSTRY, 1990–2005

1. Tell me about the information given in the graph. (60 seconds)
2. What do you think might be some of the reaons for the changes represented in the graph above? (60 seconds)

(ETS, 2002)

Explaining the contents of a graph or explaining a process is a fairly common task in many professional and study settings. To do well on the task, the speakers need to set the scene and identify parts of the information or stages in the process that they are explaining and present them in a coherent order. They also need to explain the significance of the important parts or stages, so that the listeners understand what the explanation is about and why it is being given. Explaining is a fairly monologic function in that there is clearly one main speaker, and the listeners do not necessarily need to react while the speaker is speaking. This is why explanation tasks are suitable for tape-based testing. Predictions go together well with explanation tasks, and they can also be fairly monologic. As predictions involve speculation, they may become more interactive in a face-to-face setting, however, as the uncertainty of speculation allows room for negotiation. In Example 8, the scope of the prediction is clearly limited by the information given in the graph. In an interactive situation, the participants might continue into what this might mean for the economy and ecology in different parts of the world, and whether the development would be similar all over the world, for example.

The task in Example 8 comes from the Test of Spoken English. It is intended for adults, and many of the examinees are applying for university entrance. The task is cognitively demanding, but it is likely to be appropriate in this setting. In school examinations, the cognitive complexity of graphs and graph-related tasks is an issue, since the intention of the task is probably to evaluate the examinees' language skills rather than their cognitive ability or their familiarity with interpreting graphs. If graphs are used in school tests, it would be a good idea to check textbooks in other subjects to see what kinds of graphs the examinees are expected to be able to read, and how much explanation the graphs require. Maths teachers may also be able to give comments on the appropriateness of possible graph tasks, and a dry run with a student or even another teacher might show the amount of preparation time that the examinees need for understanding the information in the graph before being asked to explain it.

The task in Example 8 also shows that speaking tasks can age. If the task were used continuously, it might be necessary to update the graph some time around year 2005. Graphs for explanation tasks can usually be found in magazines or books that deal with social issues, and the type of information in them is typically time-bound. This is usually not a problem in teacher-made tests, where task contents are routinely changed from year to year, but in formal tests aging of task material can be an issue. In any case, if graphs are used, the developers need to keep an eye out for appropriate graphs whenever they read and, as with other pictures, it would be a good idea to try the task out before actual use in a test. A particular point to check with graphs is complexity, as many graphs are too complex for examinees to understand under stressful test settings. Appropriate graphs contain enough information to give material for a sustained explanation, but not too much, so that they are easy enough to interpret. A colleague who has not seen the draft task before can be used to check the appropriateness of a prospective graph for explanation.

Decision tasks

Here is an example of a decision task for a pair of examinees.

Example 9: Task card for two examinees in a paired interview

Attending trade fairs

Your company has been invited to take part in a trade fair, which will take place during the busiest time of the year. You have been asked to decide whether staff should be sent to this trade fair.

Discuss and decide together:

- what the advantages and disadvantages are of attending trade fairs
- which members of staff would most usefully represent a company at a trade fair

(UCLES, 2001c)

Decision tasks involve discussing the issue that the decision concerns from a number of perspectives and then making a decision. In speaking tests, the issues that need to be decided are usually not clear-cut, so that arguments for and against different solutions are needed. The speakers express their opinions about the concerns and justify them in order to air different viewpoints before negotiating the conclusion. They need to follow the discussion and tie their own turns to those of the others. Decision tasks are fundamentally interactive, and if a version of this task is used in tape-based testing the task becomes one of expressing an opinion and justifying it. Interaction additionally involves negotiation between different viewpoints and taking others into account.

To develop decision tasks, task designers need to identify issues that are relevant to the examinees so that they can discuss them. Example 9 comes from the Cambridge Business English Certificate, which is intended for adults. The content and cognitive complexity of the task have been designed for this target audience. With school-age examinees, the task might involve giving advice to a young person who has written to an advice column, choosing a destination for a class trip, or deciding five things to take to a desert island. As in Example 9, it may be useful to guide the discussion with a couple of prompts, so that the task is clear for all the examinees and so that they understand that some discussion is necessary before they reach a conclusion.

Role-plays and simulations

Role-plays simulate different kinds of communication situations that the target group of the test could plausibly meet outside the test. They can be completed between two examinees or between an examinee and a tester. Example 10 comes from a paired interaction test for junior secondary-school pupils, and accordingly it is fairly generic rather than profession-specific.

Example 10: A paired interaction task*

Pupil A's test booklet

A British diplomat and his/her family stationed in Finland will be travelling in the Greek archipelago for 3 months in the summer. They are looking for a young Finn to take care of their sons (4 and 9). The diplomat father/mother, Mr/Mrs Right, is interviewing you. Try to give as good an impression as possible of yourself in this job interview.

TELL HIM/HER:
• why you want this job
• about your experience in taking care of children
• about your language skills
• that you can swim very well

ASK:
• about the nature of the job
• about working hours
• about salary, free time
• about opportunities for sailing

Pupil B's test booklet

You are a British diplomat with a wife/husband. You have two boys (4 and 9). You are going to Greece on vacation, and you need a Finnish au pair, whom you are interviewing.

START:
• by introducing yourself (you are Mr/Mrs Right)
• by asking the interviewee's name

ASK:
• why he/she is applying for the job
• experience
• swimming ability
• language skills

PROMISE:
• a pleasant job
• beautiful scenery
• good salary
• nice, well-behaved children
• to let the applicant know the following day

FINISH THE INTERVIEW POLITELY by stating that you have another meeting coming up.

REMEMBER to say goodbye.

* translated from Finnish original

Unlike in most role-play tasks, Pupil B in Example 10 is being asked to play a role that they would not normally have. This can create grave difficulties in tests, since acting ability can influence the performance unfairly. Therefore, in high-stake tests, the examiners usually play the roles that are not familiar or likely to the examinees. The teacher who used this task with her students knew from her classroom experience that the students had done this before and were used to it. Still, the instructions for this role in the test booklet are quite detailed in order to make it easier for the students to play it. The task comes from the test that was discussed as Example 1 in Chapter 6.

Role-play tasks are a way of making communication in a test more versatile because, rather than talking to a tester, the examinees take on a new role and a new, simulated role relationship to their communication partner. Their performance shows their ability to adapt to the requirements of the new role and situation. As long as the situation is relevant for the target audience and the purpose of the test, this gives useful information for the tester. The information may simply be a new perspective into the examinees' linguistic resources, or the task may involve the use of different functions from other tasks in the test. Depending on the rating criteria, the talk may also be evaluated from a task or situation-based perspective, as ability to deal with the situation being simulated.

Simulated situation tasks are very similar to role-plays in that they involve acting out an imagined communication situation. Example 11 comes from a tape-based test of academic English, the CAEL Oral Language Test, which was introduced in Chapter 6.

The simulation in the CAEL OLT is fairly extended. In this task, the examinees have to imagine they are taking a course, and the test booklet contains a handout from one of the lessons. From the tape, the examinees hear a listening extract from the class in which the teacher gives them a small group presentation task. The teacher's talk makes it clear that the class has already been divided into three-member teams. The tape continues with the beginning of the small group discussion, where the examinees hear the two other members of the examinee's team present their plans for their sections of the presentation. The team members then ask the examinee to choose one of the remaining topics and talk about it.

Example 11: A tape-based test

Examinee's test booklet

In this task you will be asked to participate in a group discussion.

HANDOUT: on violence in society

Your group will give an oral presentation on each of the following aspects of violence in society. Each member of the group should choose one topic listed below.

Choose your topic from the list below

TOPIC	DETAILS
Violence in movies	effect on children
	effect on male/female relationship
Violence in families	effect on children
	problems with elderly people
Violence in schools	effect on learning
	weapon control in high schools
Violence on the streets	effect on ordinary citizens
	cost for police, etc.

Transcribed extract from the listening input for the task

Listen to your team members start the discussion.

Female: okay so ehh . I dunno about you but ehh the topic I'd really like to do I think is violence in the movies

Male: okay

Female: emm I think you know . it's something that occurred to me it's you know this eh this recent Star Wars . eh movie

Male: mhmm yeah

Female: that is coming out and eh . and you know you think of how often . people are troubling each other shooting each other

Male: that's true

Female: you know it's like . violence is the only . [solution to a problem]

Male: [it seems like it] . yeah

Female: and I . worry about that you know you . think of all the kids that watch that in cartoons you know

Male: sure

Female: movies and I'm sure that there has been some research that suggests that this isn't a problem . but I think .. I think it IS a problem and I'd really like to look into that . eh and it's not only kids it's also the way genders are . are displayed like you know the male/female relationships you know . . .

(© CAEL, 2000, reprinted with permission)

The construct definition in the CAEL OLT is context-based, relating to speaking skills that are needed in academic studies. The task in Example 11 tests listening and responding to group discussions, elaborating or extending an idea in one's own words, defining key terms in one's own words, and telling a story from one's own experience to support a point (CAEL, 2000). The informal style of the voices on the tape invites the examinees to use similar, spoken-like talk in their performance and shows that a formal presentation style is not needed.

Since all the tasks in a version of the CAEL OLT relate to a single theme, the test developers need to take this into account when writing new versions of this task. They need to find a topic that is appropriate for a beginning university class and write a group project worksheet for it. They then need to develop materials for the tape. To avoid talk that is too written-like, they might write outlines for the speakers who will play the group members, rather than actual lines that they should speak. Next, the recordings will be made, with possibly a few practice takes to make the discussion flow naturally. One speaker will act as 'the course teacher' and two others, preferably a male and a female, as group members. Then, the examinee booklets and the master tape are put together and tried out before actual use in a test. For a different tape-based simulation task, a similar generic task structure would need to be created and then filled with actual contents much as in this example.

Simulations can also be used in face-to-face tests. This is very typical of profession-specific language tests such as the Occupational English Test (see McNamara, 1996), which tests medical professionals' ability to deal with professional communication in English. Simulation allows the testers to standardise and control the assessment event. This is useful not only in specific purpose assessment but also in professionally specific learning environments, as Example 12 shows.

Example 12: Teacher's activity plan

Lesson 1

Introduce the assessment activity. Pairs of students will be giving a factory tour of a paper mill and a wood processing plant.

Ask class to reflect on 'What makes a good factory tour?'

- Work on your own for 10 minutes. Make notes.
- Work together in small groups. Draw a mind map.

Summarise results on whiteboard.

View factory tour video.

What was good about this tour? What could have been done better?

Ask students to select a partner to work with.

Write down the names of pairs and prepare the chart for conducting the test.

Lessons 2–4
Students will:

- Make a production chart for their paper mill and wood processing plant on the basis of materials they bring to class.
- Conduct an audience analysis, following the framework they learned in their mother tongue lessons, and plan manuscripts for the two tours that they will give.
- Rehearse their presentation so they will not need to read too much from written notes.
- Give their production charts and manuscripts to the teacher for feedback and make changes based on the discussion.
- Rehearse on location to check timing (15 minutes) and the appropriateness of their tours.

Lesson 5
The simulated tours are conducted. Pairs of students act as hosts and guests. The teacher circulates between the groups, observing each pair for 2–3 minutes. Immediately after each tour, the students fill in self- and peer-evaluation forms.

Lesson 6
Conduct a general feedback discussion with the whole class.

Ask students to review their notes and add explanations if needed. Collect peer feedback.

Conduct short feedback discussions with each pair.

The assessment design in Example 12 is situation-based. The learners are future wood and paper engineers, so giving factory tours is a relevant task for them. The task requires the learners to give presentations and interact professionally as hosts and guests. In their preparation and performance, the learners need to accommodate their language use to the simulated situation (expertise of audience in the process being presented, time available, noise level, etc.). Although simulated, the task is relatively demanding in terms of ability to convey messages comprehensibly under realistic conditions (information structuring, audience accommodation, comprehensibility over noise), and it requires the use of professional vocabulary. The students work in pairs, however, and they are allowed to practise the tours without an audience before the actual assessment situation. This simulates collaboration between colleagues in non-test situations, and the requirement to assess self and peers encourages the development of skills in constructive peer assessment and reflection/self-assessment.

Task development in learning-related assessments such as Example 12 puts the teacher in the role of a guide and a communication consultant. He or she has to plan the simulated task and the evaluation criteria, but keep both designs open so that the details can be decided collaboratively with the students. The teacher also has to provide material for the students so that they can extract the significant features of the task and performances from them. In Example 12, the brainstorming activity and the videotape of factory tours in Lesson 1 served this purpose. As Example 12 shows, learning-related assessment blends together with the learning aims of the course.

Simulations and role-plays allow the test developers to use different ways of defining the skills that are being assessed in the tasks. They can choose linguistically oriented concepts such as vocabulary, grammar and pronunciation, but they can also use communication-oriented concepts such as getting the message across and using appropriate strategies, or they can choose the situation and speaker role as the main concepts. In the context of Example 12, they might talk about the examinees' skills in English for engineering, specifically related to giving factory tours or, in the context of Example 11, the examinees' skills in academic English. This flexibility is a clear advantage of simulations and role-plays as speaking assessment tasks.

Reacting in situations tasks

Reacting in situations tasks combine some of the features of simulations and function-based communication tasks. Example 13 shows the beginning of one such task.

Example 13: A tape-based test

Examinee's test booklet
In this task, you are asked to give appropriate responses in English to the situations described below. You will first be given some time to read through the description of the situation – you will hear a request to 'look at Situation

1'. Then you will hear the prompt: 'Start speaking now, please', which is followed by a pause. During this pause, you should give your response. The length of the pause is indicated in parentheses after each task.

Situation 1

An English colleague has been working with you and sharing your workspace. Yesterday your supervisor told you that she believes your colleague has been using your phone to make personal calls to the UK. Your supervisor asks you to inform your colleague about the office policy of using the phones for company business only, although local calls are fine. What do you say to your colleague? (30 sec)

Situation 2

You are meeting a friend at the Amsterdam Airport. His plane from London seems to be an hour late and the Information Board is not working any more. You go to an airport official and ask for news of your friend's flight. What do you say? (25 sec)

(© National Certificates, 2003, reprinted with permission)

The mini-simulations of reacting in situations can be used in tape-based and live tests. The advantage over longer simulations is that the testers get a more versatile impression of the examinees' skills as they can fit a range of language-use situations into a couple of minutes. The main design consideration is the kinds of situations and functions that the testers want to know about. The situations may also include social complications, as in Example 13, to test the examinees' ability to adapt their talk to them and use strategies to get their message across smoothly. This type of language use is quite difficult to cover in interview-type discussion. Since the task usually includes a handful of different situations, it fits tape-based testing better anyway, as it is difficult for a tester to change roles credibly too many times. It is artificial in that no communication situation outside the test would normally require as many changes of role and context in such quick succession, but from another perspective it makes efficient use of the already contrived testing situation, while the situation descriptions make it seem fairly realistic to examinees in terms of communication.

Structured speaking tasks

Structured speaking tasks are called 'structured' because they control quite closely what the examinees are going to say. In reading aloud and sentence repetition, the testers know exactly what the examinees will say, and, in short-answer questions and reacting to phrases tasks, a short list of acceptable answers can usually be specified. Structured speaking tasks are typically used to evaluate linguistic features, particularly pronunciation and grammar. Short-answer questions and reactions to phrases can also be used to evaluate overall understanding and comprehensibility.

Here is an example of a reading-aloud task.

Example 14: A telephone-mediated test

Examinee's test booklet

Part A: Reading. *Please read out the sentences as you are instructed.*

1. Traffic is a huge problem in Southern California.
2. The endless city has no coherent mass transit system.
3. Sharing rides was going to be the solution to rush-hour traffic.
4. Most people still want to drive their own cars, though.

(© Ordinate, 2002)

Here is another example of a reading-aloud task.

Example 15: A tape-based test

Examinee's test booklet

Occasionally in your academic program, you will need to read aloud, for example, to quote from sources or to refer to a part of a reading. In this task you will be asked to read the article you spoke about in the previous task.

PEI post-secondary student gets a boost

CHARLOTTETOWN. Prince Edward Island has developed new initiatives, including a $2-million award program, to help its post-secondary students.

Awards of $600 each will go to 800 third- and fourth-year students at the University of Prince Edward Island. Four hundred students in their second year at Holland College will also be eligible.

The government also announced it will delay the interest on student loans for up to 60 months in cases where graduates are either unemployed or underemployed.

(© CAEL, 2000)

Reading aloud tests different aspects of pronunciation and comprehensibility. The testers need to design the texts so that they include the kinds of intonation contours, stress and rhythm patterns, and individual sounds that they want to know about. The texts are usually not very long, and in Example 14 the instructions on the recorded telephone-mediated test actually ask the examinees to read the sentences one by one in an arbitrary order. Thus, any speaking features beyond the sentence level are not assessed in this task. Example 15 is more situation-based, and this type of reading aloud is sometimes included also in live tests. For example, two Australian tests for foreign language teachers include a reading-aloud section as a part of a role-play where the examinee reads to students in their professional role as a teacher (Brown, 2003, personal communication). In this latter type of test, reading aloud is assessed as the specific skill that it is, because this is a skill that is needed in the target situation of the test. Since pronunciation can be assessed as part of any speaking task, reading aloud is a feasible option in two contexts: in taped tests where the predictability of an examinee's talk is clearly an issue, and in cases where the whole skill of reading aloud is relevant for the target situation of the test.

Factual short-answer questions are often used in tape-based tests and sometimes also in role-plays on a live test. The examinees usually read a text that contains the information asked for in the task, and then they hear questions to which they have to reply. Example 16 shows one such task from a tape-based test of Japanese for tourism and hospitality.

Example 16: A tape-based test

Examinee's test booklet

You are asked for information on suburban train travel. From the details below, reply to the question.

    Full day travelcard $3.00
    Three hour travelcard $1.50

(Adapted from Brown, 1993)

An extract from the tape transcript

Instructor   You are asked for information on suburban train travel. First read the information in your booklet. You will then be asked the question.

(5 sec)

Client   Kippu wa ikura desu ka? [How much is the ticket?]

(15 sec)

(Adapted from Brown, 1993)

Short-answer questions test comprehension of the questions and ability to give relevant information in response. The difference between this and more extended simulations is that the questions and answers are limited and all the information needed for answering the questions is usually provided in the task materials. If the text is written in the target language, the task only requires finding the information and relaying it in spoken form. If, as in Example 16, the information is not in the test language, the examinees also need to find the right words to use. The task may require simple reporting of the information or, as in Example 16, the examinees may need to give a slightly longer explanation, in this case specifying two categories of ticket prices. The answers are usually evaluated for linguistic accuracy, content accuracy and, possibly, appropriateness for the situation.

Reacting to phrases is another structured task that is often used in tape-based tests. The task usually tests the examinees' knowledge of conventional politeness exchanges such as greetings, thanks, apologies, expressions of agreement and polite disagreement, and so on. Two examples of this task type are shown below.

Example 17: A tape-based test of Japanese for tourism and hospitality

Extract from the test information sheet

This section tests the ability to understand and use courtesy formulae. Candidates will hear 6 remarks in Japanese, such as greetings, thanks, apologies, complaints, etc., which are likely to be made in a variety of occupational situations when dealing with Japanese clients.

Examples:

Okurete sumimasen. (Sorry to be late.)

Kireina machi desu ne! (Isn't this a pretty town!)

(Adapted from Brown, 1993)

Example 18: A tape-based test

Sample tape transcript

Task 1

First, you will hear a number of remarks which might be made to you in various situations when you are speaking English. Some are questions and some are comments. After each one, reply in a natural way.

Here is an example:

> Sorry to keep you waiting.
> That's all right.

Now, are you ready? Here is the first.

1. Where've you been? We started ten minutes ago.
2. It's hot in here.
3. Didn't you see the red light?

(Weir, 1993: 49)

The examinee responses are usually evaluated for their intelligibility and appropriateness. Since basic social politeness is an important aspect of speaking skills in any language, this task type is often included in tape-based proficiency tests for basic and intermediate skill levels. In advanced levels, the more complicated reacting in situations task is usually used instead. To develop the prompts, the task designers need to consider which social formulae are important to test, and then write and record the first turn of the pair. As with other taped tasks, the appropriateness of the answer times needs to be checked and, at the same time, the test developers can sample the range of answers that the tasks are likely to elicit.

Practical issues in task design

Choosing what to test

While the choice of what to test is a practical issue in task design, it is also directly linked to the issue of construct definition as discussed in Chapter 6. In practice, this means choosing the concepts that the developers use when they think and talk about the test. In this book, I have talked about three main frameworks for defining the construct: linguistically oriented, communication-oriented and situation-based.

The concepts that the developers use in linguistically oriented definitions are typically vocabulary, grammar and pronunciation. If the developers choose this framework, they use these concepts to plan the tasks. They may combine this with planning the functions (such as apologising or explaining) and topic areas that are covered. Language use is often analysed in learning materials in this way, so this may be the most familiar approach to teachers.

Communication-oriented concepts for task planning include those discussed in Examples 1–9 in this chapter. The first level of definition is the overall communication activity in the task, such as telling a narrative or expressing and defending an opinion. The main planning concepts, then, are the features that make the communication of this macro-function successful. With narratives, for example, the task should require setting the scene, identifying the characters and referring to them consistently, identifying the main events, and telling them in a coherent sequence. With expressing and defending opinions, the tasks should require (and possibly provide materials for) expressing an opinion on an issue, contrasting it with other possible opinions, and discussing factors that support the chosen opinion and argue against others. The examinee performances may also be evaluated in terms of these concepts, possibly in combination with delivery features such as engagingness or fluency. I will discuss evaluation criteria in Chapter 8.

Situation-based task design belongs to the task-based approach to defining the test construct, as discussed in Chapter 6. This approach is typically used in specific-purpose testing and in vocational and professional education. The planning starts from the examinees' communication needs in the target situation. The actual concepts used in task design may vary. Sometimes it is enough that the tasks make the examinees use relevant language to fulfil their role. At other times the testers want the examinees to simulate all aspects of their professional life. The task instructions must make it clear how the examinees should approach the task.

The decision about the concepts used in task design is largely made on the basis of the purpose of the test and the context in which it is used. The test users need some information, and the test provides it, but sometimes the type of information that is needed is not specified in detail. In this case, the test developers have a chance to influence, possibly even educate, the test users. Linguistically oriented concepts are the most traditional, and test users may know them simply because of this. The evaluation concepts related to communicative functions or situations may be newer to them, but possibly no less relevant. Many teachers, in fact, may need to think about whether their design principles for teaching and evaluation match each other. Communication-orientated or situation-based concepts may be closer to the current thinking in language education.

Teachers and testers can, of course, also combine all three approaches in their work. The purpose of one test or task may be to provide a limited piece of very specific information, for example on the examinees' pronunciation accuracy. The purpose of another test, with a range of tasks, may be to provide an overall picture of the examinees' skill level at the time of testing. The choice of concepts for task design thus depends on the purpose and scope of the test.

Writing task specifications

Task specifications are a document that test developers use when they design new versions of a test or task. They also use them to check whether a task they have developed covers the skills it was supposed to cover. Task specifications contain the test instructions, definitions related to each task and the materials needed for implementing them, and an overview of test administration plans. The development of instructions and administration plans was discussed in Chapter 6.

The task-by-task definitions specify the skills that will be assessed and the task materials needed for assessing them. They also characterise the structure and approximate length of each task and often include an example to show what the definitions mean in practice.

Task specifications are equivalent to blueprints of industrial products, and maybe for this reason they are very rarely published. I have extrapolated the specifications below on the basis of my work experience with tests. The task is Example 2 from the beginning of this chapter, where two examinees are asked to describe their pictures to each other.

Example 19: Task specifications for the description task in Example 2

Task 2: Describing pictures

Communication	pair work between two examinees
Expected duration	2 minutes
Skills to be assessed	giving physical descriptions of views and objects, specifying locations of objects in a picture, asking and answering questions, identifying similarities and differences
Appropriate topics	views/scenery, town scenes, buildings, rooms. The pictures should have some people in them.
Task materials	– 2 line drawings – examiner outline (generic) – 3–4 support questions in case the examinees stop too soon. They should talk for approximately 2 minutes.

The task is based on two line drawings, which are similar but not the same. The drawings should have something in the foreground, three to four things in the middle, and something in the background. All the main objects or parts in both pictures should belong to the same category, but the details in them should be different. See example below.

[the two pictures from Example 2 would go here]

Support questions: *describe the scenery, describe the town, what part of the world* . . .

Examiner outline

In this part of the test, I will give each of you a picture. Don't show the pictures to each other.

Hand over the pictures.

Please describe your pictures to each other and then talk about what is similar in your pictures and what is different. Student A, you begin.

If necessary, ask them further questions.

Although task specifications logically come first and task writing second, this is not really what happens in practice. Rather, test developers often begin with an initial idea of what will be included in a task, and they draft the specifications together with one or two versions of the actual task. Sometimes they may not write specifications at all, or they may write them afterwards, but it is always a good idea to write them. Most speaking tests require the use of parallel tasks because the tests are so often administered individually or in pairs and the tester does not want information about the test contents to spread. It is much easier to write parallel tasks with the help of task specifications, which define the key features of the task. They also provide criteria for evaluating the quality of draft tasks.

Writing the actual task materials and tasks

Even with the help of task specifications, task writing is a craft. The developers need to find appropriate topics and scenarios, imagine the communication during the actual testing situation, and create all the materials that are needed when the task is actually used. In the course of writing more tasks and trying them out, the developers often find that specifications can be improved. Whenever this happens, it is a good idea to make the modifications straight away. However salient an insight seems when the developer is working on a task, it is soon forgotten once he or she starts to work with something else. Experience-based, revised specifications are very helpful for future task writing.

The first drafts of tasks are always just that, first drafts. The central idea for a task may remain the same throughout the development, but the task as a whole can usually be improved through reflection and re-reading, comments from other people, and revisions. Colleagues can be especially useful as commentators, because they know the testing context. However, any second pair of eyes on a task or interview protocol in addition to the writer's is better than none. In other words, task writing is group work, and discussion helps writers distance themselves from their drafts and thereby possibly improve them.

If it is possible to try out a new set of tasks, even with one or a few language learners who are similar to the real examinees, this will provide highly useful feedback about task implementation. In the case of tape-based tests, trialling is almost obligatory because the instructions and answer times may need to be adjusted. Since tape-based assessment often implies formal testing, usually of large groups of examinees, it is important to get the technical implementation right to ensure that the scores reflect the desired aspects of speaking ability instead of, say, ability to cope with overly long or short answer times. With tasks that are given interactively, small-scale trialling will show the kinds of strategies that will be needed when introducing the task into the assessment interaction. When the teacher, task writer and tester are one and the same person, a dry run will help the tester prepare for the real testing situation and thus possibly make the first examinee's test more similar to other examinees' tests than it would be without practice. In formal interview-based tests, this familiarisation forms part of interlocutor training. The trialling of tasks is done earlier in the development of the assessment protocols that the interlocutors will use.

In some contexts, it is possible to keep changing the test for every new implementation. In others, it is necessary to wait to make revisions, because standardisation and test comparability across different test dates are important for the way in which the scores are used. The principle of learning from practice and making the assessment resemble intentions as well as possible is an underlying theme in both cases. Speaking tasks are practical tools that are not perfect, but with good planning and at least some revisions they can provide good evidence of the examinees' speaking skills.

Selecting and creating pictures for tasks

The design of speaking tasks may sometimes start from a picture, but usually the developers have a basic idea first, and then, if the idea involves pictures they start to look for or create them. If the task idea is very specific, it is usually easier to create the picture specifically. The format may be line drawings, photographs or computer graphics; the point is that the pictures need to serve the purpose of the task. They have to generate the type of talk that the developers are after, whether that is description, narrative, negotiated interpretation, or whatever. One easy way of checking this is to try the pictures out before using them for real. This should happen early enough so there is still time to find or create new pictures if some of them do not work.

One reason why pictures are used as task materials is that they evoke meanings and ideas without using actual words that might influence the examinees' performance too strongly. Pictures are also often quicker than written task materials, so they save testing time. There is always some ambiguity about pictures, however, and as a rule of thumb it is a good idea to make test pictures clear enough so that they do not intimidate the examinees by their visual complexity. Purposefully ambiguous pictures are a special case, as the intention is usually to make the examinees hypothesise about the intended message. These are appropriate for assessing hypothetical language, but there may be a need for a back-up solution to make sure that it is not picture interpretation but the language demands of the task that make the task difficult for some examinees. In tests with an interlocutor, the script should probably provide support questions in case an examinee is at a loss for ideas to talk about.

Another possible danger with pictures, especially maps or graphs, is cognitive complexity. The intention is usually to test the examinees' language skills, not their ability to read graphs or maps, which means that maps in particular are usually specially created for the test. However, if the map or graph is too simple, the danger is that it may not generate enough talk. One way of checking the appropriateness of the cognitive demands of a picture task is to ask some mock examinees to perform it in their mother tongue and make adjustments if necessary.

Humour is always welcome in tests but, as mentioned in Chapter 3, humorous pictures or picture sequences such as cartoons do not automatically make good testing material. They may generate too little talk, or the visual humour may be difficult to express in words. Again, trying the task out before actual use in a test should reveal my potential problems.

Tape-mediated and face-to-face tasks

This chapter has included examples of both tape-based and live speaking tasks. The task development differences between them are not necessarily great except in one sense, namely that the input in tape-based tests is much more standardised and it must be designed and recorded beforehand. In face-to-face testing, the same degree of standardisation is only possible if the examiners are given exact lines that they should speak and are required to use them. This is done in some cases, but more often the talk that the examinees hear is somewhat unpredictable. From the perspective of test comparability across examinees, this is not a good thing. From the perspective of natural communication, however, it is, in the sense that speakers usually accommodate their talk according to previous turns in the discourse. The lack of reciprocity in tape-based testing can seem artificial to the examinees. If examination developers go for a tape-mediated test, they may choose to exploit the artificial context and pack the test full of different communication tasks. They may also choose to simulate interactive communication as far as the medium allows, as in Example 11 above.

From a practical perspective, the creation of tape-mediated assessments requires a recording, editing and trialling process with the tape to make sure that the test will run as smoothly as possible. In face-to-face testing, the corresponding work involves training interlocutors and making sure that their scripts work, and it is important for assessment developers to realise that both these processes will take time.

The language of task instructions

As the examples in this chapter have shown, speaking tasks sometimes include long and detailed instructions and verbal prompts. The language of these requires careful thought. If the material is given in the examinees' mother tongue, there is a danger that they will translate it directly, leading to odd or stilted language use simply because of the task design. If it is given in the target language, the examinees can pick up words and expressions from the prompts and string them together to form an acceptable response without needing to generate the response themselves. The issue is especially important in structured tasks, where the responses are usually short and clearly guided. With these, prompts in the target language usually work better, because it minimises continuous, artificial switching between languages. With more extended tasks, the issue is more open, and trials can clarify which language works better. Sometimes there is no choice, as the examinees represent too many mother tongues. In this case, it is important to keep the instructions and prompts simpler than the expected performance of the examinees, since support materials should provide support rather than make the task more difficult.

Summary

In this chapter, I have given examples of speaking tasks and discussed some central themes in task development work and the writing of task specifications. The main point in designing tasks is the information that the test users need, which guides the choice of the types of tasks to be included and the words used for describing the tasks. These concepts also lie at the basis of the rating criteria to be used, and these will be discussed in Chapter 8.

CHAPTER EIGHT

Ensuring a reliable and valid speaking assessment

From a testing perspective, speaking is special because of its interactive nature. It is often tested in live interaction, where the test discourse is not entirely predictable, just as no two conversations are ever exactly the same even if they are about the same topic and the speakers have the same roles and aims. There is also some variability in the rating process because it involves human raters. This means that special procedures are needed to ensure the reliability and validity of the scores. In this chapter, I will provide an overview of these procedures. This topic closes the cycle of speaking assessment, and in the course of the discussion I will revisit some of the main themes of this book. I will conclude the chapter with a look forward into future developments in speaking assessment.

The importance of rating in the speaking assessment cycle

The development and use of speaking tests is a cyclical process. It starts from a need for speaking scores and finishes with the use of the scores for this purpose. In between, there is a test development process and a two-step testing process, where the test is first administered and then scored. The administration is an interaction between the examinees and interlocutors or other examinees to complete the tasks, and it produces the test discourse. The rating is an interaction between the raters, the criteria and the performances included in the test discourse to produce the scores.

The focus in designing speaking assessments is often on the tasks. They are important because the examinees' experience of the test is based on them, but the validity of the scores depends equally much on the rating criteria and the relationship between the criteria and the tasks. If the criteria are developed in isolation long after the tasks have been finalised, as they often are, there is a danger of a mismatch, which leads to a loss of information about the quality of the performance (Grove and Brown, 2001). The development of rating criteria was discussed in Chapter 4. However, to put the criteria into practice, the rating process also needs to be planned with care in order to ensure the meaningfulness of the scores.

Designing the rating process

The rating process determines exactly how the criteria will be applied to the performances. Do the raters rate the performances task by task? Do they pay attention to all the criteria on all tasks, or should they use some criteria on some tasks and other criteria on others? If both holistic and analytic criteria are used, which rating should they give first? These practical decisions clarify the meaning of the criteria, and the process design may lead the developers to make some further modifications to them.

The decisions about the rating process are guided by the structure of the test and the definition of the test construct. Tape-based and highly structured live tests often contain short responses, which are generally scored one by one. The points are added up into task or section scores and total scores, e.g. 13/20 or 35/40, which may be converted into band scores for reporting. To make this kind of scoring fair, the test developers need to make sure that the effort spent on earning each point is approximately equal, that the weighting between tasks is fair, and that the skills needed to earn the points are relevant for the construct that the test is intended to assess.

Live tests that are clearly divided into tasks are also often scored task by task, but the length of the performances usually warrants the use of scales rather than score points. The scales are often task-specific, or different combinations of a generic set of scales may be used with different tasks. Thus, a monologic description task might be scored for comprehensibility, discourse organisation, accuracy and fluency, while a discussion task that follows it might be scored for interaction skills, appropriateness and vocabulary range. The aim is to evaluate the most salient performance features on each task. If there is an overall grade, it is usually derived by averaging the task scores and using judgement to decide whether to round it up or down, but sometimes some criterion or task may be explicitly weighted more heavily than others. This would be appropriate when the criterion or task is particularly important for the purpose of the test.

The raters might also be asked to listen to the entire performance and only give their rating(s) at the end but, especially if there is only one holistic rating, such a process leaves very few traces about what the rater observed in the performance and how he or she arrived at the score. This is why raters are usually asked to make detailed ratings even if only an overall score is reported. Some or all of the detailed scoring information may also be reported to the examinees as feedback.

To gather the detailed rating information, test developers need to design a **rating form** for their test. This is the concrete form that the raters use to record their ratings. The form usually concerns one examinee at a time to help the rater focus on the performance in hand and compare it against the criteria rather than using other examinees' performances as comparison points. The examinee's and raters names are filled in at the top of the form, after which the form lists the criteria in the order in which the ratings must be made. If the performances are rated task by task, for example, the form might have the headings *Task 1: Description* and the criteria used for rating it, followed by *Task 2: Discussion* and the criteria that must be used with that task. If rating scales are used, the numbers or letters corresponding to the levels are usually written on the form so that the raters only need to circle the relevant one. The scales may also be printed on the form in full, but more commonly they are provided on a separate page, because they would take up too much space on the form and make it cluttered. The form may also include space for the raters to make specific comments about the performance or about their rationale for giving a certain score. This is often a good idea because the comments are useful, for example if it turns out that two raters disagree about a rating and adjudication is needed. Sometimes the notes are also used as a basis for giving the examinees individualised feedback about their performance.

Rating forms are the concrete result of the design of the rating process. They help structure the process, speed it up, and make it consistent. Together with the wordings of scale descriptors, rating forms define what the raters pay attention to during the rating. Well-designed forms ensure that the intended features of talk are assessed, and they provide the rating information for reporting in a practical way.

Reporting scores and giving feedback

Speaking scores are usually reported as overall grades in terms of numbers or letters. These are used for decision-making, such as qualifying examinees for employment or education, giving grades, or placing students on courses, and if that is the only purpose of the test, overall grades may be the only scoring information that is reported. In learning-oriented settings, the overall grade serves as an introduction to more detailed feedback. This may be given in terms of separate ratings on analytic features such as intelligibility, rhythm and intonation, grammatical accuracy, lexical range, and appropriateness of language use, for example. If a rating checklist has been used, the feedback may describe the strengths and weaknesses of examinee performances verbally in more detail.

Since speaking tests usually involve extended responses that are rated on band scales, arriving at overall grades is not a very complex process. Even if the ratings are made task by task or analytically feature by feature, the use of the same scale levels throughout the process gives a conceptual basis for combining the scores. However, if a transition needs to be made from score points to band levels, as might be the case in tape-based and other highly structured tests, the issue of deriving overall scores may be more complex. How many items can a speaker miss to still achieve the top band? And the next lower band? If there is a point on the reporting scale below which the performance is considered a fail, how many score points should an examinee earn to pass? This issue is known as **setting cut scores**, because it involves cutting the raw score scale into ranges that correspond to the band scores.

One way to set the cut score for the passing grade is to identify a group of examinees who are known (through information that is independent of their test performance) to meet the passing criterion on the test, ask them to take the test, and see how well they do. If their performance is compared against that of another group, who are independently known to be below the passing criterion for the test, the latter group's performance should be worse, and some principled decision can be made about where between the two groups' scores the cut score should be. This principle can be followed to set cut scores for all the bands of the scale. However, it can be very difficult to find groups of examinees that are independently known to be at certain levels.

An alternative approach is to ask expert judges to look at the items and decide how well examinees at different levels should do on them. The experts should be trained professionals with relevant work experience, and they should know the scale and the intended examinees very well. With items that are scored correct/incorrect, they can be asked to estimate the probability with which an examinee at a certain level would get each item correct but, because speaking items are often scored 0/1/2 or 0/1/2/3, the use of percentages is difficult. Instead, the experts might be asked to look at items within a task or a test section and estimate how well the examinees at different score levels would do on the group of items. This process relies heavily on the accuracy and expertise of the experts, and since it is work-intensive it is only really viable for large examination boards. However, the principle of trying to apply an external criterion when setting cut scores is valid also for smaller-scale settings. Arbitrary percentages such as 50% or 60% do not have any independent meaning; only a consideration of the content of the items in relation to the skills of the examinees is going to lead to meaningful decisions about score boundaries.

In the criterion-referenced testing literature, the term used for setting cut scores is standard setting. The methods discussed in the literature are more appropriate for paper-based items than speaking tests, but some of them can be adapted for speaking if neither of the methods above is practical in a specific setting. For further examples of standard setting methods, see e.g. Popham (1990) or Brown and Hudson (2002).

In addition to overall scores, the test developers may want to report more detailed feedback to the examinees. This is particularly common in classroom assessment. According to Wiggins (1998), feedback that supports learning describes the performance in concrete terms, relating it to the task instructions and descriptions of expectations about good or acceptable task performance. Effective feedback may concentrate on weaknesses more than strengths, but it can be helpful when coupled with concrete descriptions about better performance. For good learners, teachers may need to give examples or descriptions of performances on other, more advanced tasks, so that they, too, can set themselves new learning goals. This type of descriptive feedback makes the rating process more understandable to the examinees, and with time it can change the concepts and strategies they use in evaluating their own performance.

Feedback can also be based on detailed specifications of learning goals (Brown and Hudson, 2002). The goals must be specified concretely, however, as for example in 'tell a story involving three characters in a way that is easy to follow, setting the scene appropriately, narrating a sequence of events, and making consistent reference to the characters'. If a list of such speaking goals can be specified, feedback throughout the course or the year can be given in terms of how well each learner meets the goal at various stages. A feedback form that the students get in the middle or at the end of a course can contain assessments from earlier stages as well, so that they can see their own progress. Teachers can use the same feedback form to evaluate the performance of the whole class if they average the student scores on each objective at each evaluation point. They can then identify areas that have been learned adequately by the group and others that may need more attention.

Giving detailed feedback takes time, and in education this is often in short supply. However, if a teacher has taken the time to define the learning goals and arrange a speaking assessment, and if the rating process provides material for detailed feedback, it would be a waste of effort not to use it. Students are also usually interested in learning what the teacher or rater thought about their performance. A well-structured rating form can increase the efficiency of feedback sessions, and combining the feedback with advice for further learning makes the time spent on giving feedback more useful for both teachers and students.

Feedback does not have to be a unidirectional procedure from the evaluator to the evaluated. Students, teachers, administrators, and whoever else receives feedback about the test results can be included in score interpretation and the drawing of implications from them. Students may have insights about tasks, criteria, test administration procedures, or the importance of some of the learning goals for their personal progress, and they can be asked about that when the feedback is still fresh in their minds. Teachers may similarly evaluate either the assessment procedures or their teaching, and they can take their proposals forward to the students and/or school administrators. In this way, evaluation becomes part of the teaching, learning and other activities that surround it.

Aiming for useful speaking scores

Like all test scores, speaking scores must be dependable, fair, and above all useful for the intended purposes. The main technical qualities that testing specialists use in this context are reliability and validity. Reliability relates to the consistency of the scores, and validity to their meaningfulness for the intended uses. In addition, the test needs to be practical in terms of resources required to arrange it. If the resource demands are too high, the test will simply not be developed or arranged, even if it has been developed.

The necessary qualities of language tests can be discussed in terms of the overarching concept of usefulness (Bachman and Palmer, 1996). The point with using this type of an overarching concept is that the qualities cannot be analysed and evaluated independently, but rather they must be considered together. For example, including a group discussion task in a test of English for university entrance might be very relevant from the point of view of correspondence between the test tasks and the target language-use situation, but for practical reasons it might be very difficult to arrange the test in this way. Thus, the more ideal task might be substituted by a discussion task between an interlocutor and an individual examinee or a simulated group discussion on a tape-based test, reducing the costs and standardising the administration process while still maintaining some of the content focus of the original task.

In the rest of this chapter, I will concentrate on the technical qualities of reliability and validity. I will treat each theme on its own but, as the discussion will show, they are closely interrelated and clearly arise from the concrete situation in which the test is arranged. A more detailed discussion of statistical procedures for reliability and validity can be found in Bachman (forthcoming).

Defining reliability for speaking assessments

Reliability is usually defined as score consistency (AERA, 1999; Brown and Hudson, 2002; Henning, 1987). If the scores from a test given today are reliable, they will remain largely the same if the test is given to the same people again tomorrow. Reliability is important because it means that the scores are dependable, so that we can rely on them in decision-making. Unreliable scores, on the other hand, can lead to wrong placements, unjustified promotions, or undeservedly low grades on report cards, for example, because the particular scores that were used to make the decisions were influenced by the circumstances of the testing occasion rather than the ability of the examinees, and they would have come out differently on another occasion.

Procedures for ensuring reliability

The reliability of speaking scores builds on high-quality scoring instruments and procedures. The methods of ensuring reliability are somewhat different for formal tests given by examination boards and for classroom tests and assessments. I will therefore discuss these separately.

Reliability assurance for formal examinations

The most common procedure that examination boards use to ensure the reliability of their scoring is rater training. Training sessions typically last several days, and they are often arranged over two or more weekends, because the raters can only attend the training when they are not working at their normal job, which is usually teaching or educational administration. Prospective raters are selected for the training on the basis of their interest in and possibly their experience of testing. At the end of the course, they usually have to go through a qualification procedure. This involves showing, through independent rating of some taped performances, that their rating performance is consistent with that of other qualified raters in the system.

Rater training sessions often begin with an introduction to the test and the criteria. Different levels on the scale are then illustrated, usually through taped performances that have been rated by experienced raters before the training. After this, the participants practise rating by viewing more taped performances. They report their scores aloud and discuss the reasons for the consensus score and any other scores that some of them might have given. This helps them learn to apply the criteria according to the conventions of the system. If there is a second training session, the participants may get rating homework between the sessions. During the next session, the scores are again discussed until consensus about the ratings is achieved. Finally, the qualifying test is arranged, either at the end of the session or as homework.

Rater training has been criticised as a form of indoctrination, as novice raters are taught to evaluate performances in the system's terms. The case can be made that training changes the individual's perception of the world, ensuring reliability (understood as equivalence of scores awarded to performances irrespective of who gives them) but providing no proof that the scoring criteria are actually valid (Fulcher, 1997). While this observation is true, it only means that the developers need to provide some evidence about the validity of the criteria, for example by showing how they are related to the construct definition, the tasks, and the kinds of skills that the speakers need outside the test. However, the use of rater training also means that the developers recognise the impossibility of giving comparable ratings without training, and they take steps to ensure comparability because they consider it important.

The tape that is used during rater training to introduce the levels of the scale is known as the **benchmark tape**. Its purpose is to illustrate the levels in concrete terms, and performances are usually selected for it when many experienced raters agree that they are clear exemplars of a certain level. Each level is usually illustrated by two or three performances, because this allows the developers to show some of the variation that can exist within a level. Apart from introducing the scale to new raters, the benchmark tape is also used to remind trained raters of the scale before they begin their rating work. If an examination uses new tasks at each new testing round, as school-leaving examinations often do, the board may compile a new benchmark tape for each new testing round. This requires getting together a team of master raters whose judgement the board is prepared to rely on, asking them to rate a range of performances, and choosing those of the performances that the members are most agreed about in their ratings.

Another reliability-enhancing procedure that examination boards often use is **standard setting**, or the setting of cut scores or other standards of success with the help of criteria that are external to the test. Methods of setting cut scores for tape-based or highly structured and itemised live speaking tests were discussed earlier in this chapter. This involved getting known masters and known non-masters (of a certain score band) to take the test in order to define the cut point between that band and the one below it, or getting experts to describe how well examinees at certain score levels, e.g. 1, 2 and 3, would do on the test tasks. Alternatively, the raters can be asked to describe the weaknesses or wrong answers that they would allow an examinee to make while still considering them to be at a certain level. These procedures help test developers explain how the test scores are related to speaking skills outside the test. The methods are work-intensive, but the results provide an anchoring for the meaning of the scores. This helps the test developers maintain the same standards through different versions of the test, which can be very important especially for formal examinations.

The reliability of ratings is also supported by ensuring the consistency of rating procedures. The most common way of doing this is using rating forms. If intra-rater or inter-rater reliability figures indicate a potential problem with a certain rater, the forms submitted by this rater can be analysed to see if there is something there to explain the inconsistency. The rater may also be flagged for re-training.

Reliability assurance for classroom assessments

Although reliability is a basic requirement for all assessments, it is a much less formal consideration with informal assessments than it is with formal tests. The groups of examinees are usually small, and this does not warrant the use of advanced statistical methods. However, the consistency of ratings is still a concern, and a rater's internal consistency can be analysed even with very small groups, as will be shown below. Scoring reliability is maintained by using consistent rating procedures, which can be supported by rating forms.

One worry that classroom assessments often raise is subjectivity. Common suggestions for reducing subjectivity include rating test performances one task at a time and trying to score performances anonymously (Brown and Hudson, 2002). These methods are very difficult to use with speaking assessments, however. Rating task by task is impractical even if raters work from tapes, and anonymity is virtually impossible because each speaker has a recognisable voice that a teacher would recognise even from an audiotape. Practically the only alternative is for the rater to reflect on his or her own rating work and consciously attempt to be just and use the criteria consistently. Focusing on the concrete features of a performance, identifying strengths and weaknesses, and comparing these against the features mentioned in the scoring criteria may be helpful. It may also be useful to re-visit the performance that was rated first after finishing the rating of the last performance in a group. This simple self-check of consistency should show whether the rater's internal standards have changed in the course of the rating work as a result of becoming more familiar with the tasks and performances.

Analysing reliability

Three types of reliability are particularly relevant for speaking assessment. The first is **intra-rater reliability** or **internal consistency**, which means that raters agree with themselves, over a period of a few days, about the ratings that they give. Since speaking assessments are based on human rating, this cannot be assumed automatically. The second is **inter-rater reliability**, which means that different raters rate performances similarly. They do not necessarily need to agree completely, as two or more raters may see the salience of different features of performances slightly differently. However, if the raters use the same criteria, their

Table 8.1 *Two sets of holistic scores*

	1st rating	2nd rating
Allan	4	4
Ben	5	5
Beverly	2	3
Cheryl	6	6
Chris	2	3
Emily	3	4
Felicity	6	6
George	4	4
John	3	2
Jonathan	2	1
Matthew	1	1
Sharon	4	3
Susan	4	5
Tom	5	4
Wendy	6	6

ratings should not be wildly different, and in principle, it should be possible for them to come to an agreement about a joint rating. Well-defined criteria help raters agree, and frequent disagreements may indicate either that some raters are not able to apply the criteria consistently or that the criteria need to be defined better. The third type of reliability that is important for speaking assessment is **parallel form reliability**. This is relevant if there are more than one test form that are meant to be interchangeable. The examinees are asked to take two or more of the different forms, and their scores are then analysed for consistency. If the scores are not consistent, the forms cannot be considered parallel – assuming of course that the raters are internally consistent. Some of the tasks within the forms may then need to be revised.

An easy, descriptive method of examining score reliability is to cross-tabulate the scores. This helps the test developers see how much agreement there is, and when the ratings do not agree exactly, how far off they are from each other. Let us assume that we have a holistic scale from 1 to 6, and each of 15 performances has been rated twice by the same rater (internal consistency). The scores from the two rounds are listed in Table 8.1.

To cross-tabulate these scores, we start by drawing a table with six rows and six columns, one for each of the score categories. We will designate the columns for the scores from the first rating round and the rows for the scores from the second rating round. To fill the table, we find the intersections of columns and rows according to the ratings that the examinees were given. For example, Allan's performance was scored 4 on the first round and 4 on the second. So we put a 1 in the square at the intersection of the fourth column and the fourth row. Ben's performance received a 5 on the first round and also a 5 on the second, so we put a 1 in the intersection of fifth column and fifth row. Beverly's performance received a 2 on the first round and 3 on the second, so we find the intersection of the second column and the third row and put a 1 there. At the end, we add up the 1s in each cell.

First rating

		1	2	3	4	5	6
Second rating	1	1	1				
	2			1			
	3		2		1		
	4			1	2	1	
	5				1	1	
	6						3

To ease the interpretation of the cross-tabulation, I have shaded the diagonal with dark grey and the squares immediately next to it with light grey. The diagonal indicates exact agreement, and as we can see, only seven of the 15 score pairs agree exactly. However, the rest of the cases are very close to the diagonal, in the lightly shaded squares. The numbers above the diagonal indicate performances that were scored one level higher in the first round than the second (four altogether), while the numbers below the diagonal indicate performances that were scored one level lower in the first rating than the second (four altogether).

As a general tendency, there seems to be more agreement at the higher end of the scale – as indicated by the number of exact agreements – than at the lower end. This may suggest that the level descriptors for the lower levels need revision to make their application more accurate. Another observation is that there are no ratings far away from the diagonal, which means that there are no cases with a difference of two or more levels between the rating rounds. If there were, it might be useful to review the performances to see why they give rise to such disparate ratings, and perhaps also go back to the scale and see if the level descriptors could be revised to help deal with similar cases in the future. In this way, the cross-tabulation of scores can help check on the level of rating agreement and begin a diagnosis of potential problems.

The most common way of expressing reliability is through **correlation**, which is a statistical indicator for the strength of relationship between variables. In our case, these variables are speaking scores. Theoretically, the values of a correlation coefficient may vary between -1 and +1. Values close to zero indicate no relationship between the two variables, while values close to +1 indicate a strong positive relationship. Thus, a score correlation value of close to 1 means that performances which are scored high in one set of ratings also receive high scores in the other set. This is desirable in reliability statistics, whereas negative values are undesirable (and also unlikely if the raters use the same rating scale). Negative values indicate an inverse relationship between the variables being compared, so that high scores in one set would correspond to low scores in the other. There is always some error in scoring, so that a perfect 1 is practically unattainable, but values in the .8 or .9 range are usually considered good while values in the .5 or .6 range are considered worryingly weak (see e.g. Butler, 1985, or Cronbach, 1990, for a more detailed explanation).

Two of the most common reliability coefficients that can be calculated for speaking scores are the Spearman rank order correlation (usually designated by the Greek letter rho, ρ) and the Pearson product–moment correlation (commonly designated as r). The Spearman ρ for the data in Table 8.1 is .89 and the Pearson r is .87. Rank order correlations are appropriate when there is a small number of examinees and when the score scale is not an equal interval scale, which means that the distance between 1 and 2 is not necessarily the same as the distance between 3 and 4. They can be calculated by hand, and the steps for doing this are explained for example in Alderson *et al.*, 1995 (pp. 278–279) and in Bachman (forthcoming). Many statistical programs also include a function for rank order correlations. The Pearson product-moment correlation is the most common correlation coefficient, and it is routinely calculated by most statistical programs. It is slightly more difficult to calculate by hand than the Spearman ρ, but the procedure is explained for example in Brown and Hudson (2002, pp. 152–162) and in Bachman (forthcoming). Both the Spearman ρ and the Pearson r can be used to calculate intra-rater, inter-rater and parallel form reliability.

Teachers may calculate reliability coefficients for some of their class-room tests to monitor the quality of the scores. In formal testing, reliability analyses are obligatory, because the boards need to report them to help score users estimate the degree of confidence they can place on the test. To make the information more interpretable, testing boards can conduct a further simple analysis, the **standard error of measurement** (SEM). With the help of this statistic, the test developers can report reliability in terms of a confidence band around the examinee scores. For example, the score user's manual for the Test of Spoken English (ETS, 2002: 9) reports that the standard error of measurement for TSE scores is approximately plus or minus 4 points on the reporting scale. Thus, if person A has gained a score of 55 on a particular TSE administration, his or her **true score**, or the score he or she would gain on average if he or she took the test an infinite number of times, would be between 51 and 59 most of the time. The higher the reliability of an assessment and the bigger the group of examinees, the smaller the SEM becomes. The calculation of the SEM is explained for example in Brown and Hudson (2002), or in Cronbach (1990) or many other educational measurement textbooks.

The SEM shows how far it is worth taking the reported score at face value. This can be important especially if individuals are compared on the basis of their scores. If one has a score of 28 and the other a score of 31, the SEM can indicate whether the difference between them is as clear as it may seem. This also applies to band scores, for example a range from 1 to 6. If the scoring is reliable, the SEM can be a fraction of a band score, for example .34. If it is more than one score band, the reliability of the scoring is in need of improvement, as it is only possible to say that the examinee's true score is two levels above or below a score that they received. On a scale of 6 levels, this amount of variation is too much.

It is relatively rare to see the SEM reported for speaking assessments. One explanation might be that reporting it breaks the illusion of accuracy that people have about test scores. At the same time, however, the SEM helps the assessment developers share the responsibility for score variation with score users, as they cannot say that they did not know. It is also a useful quality check for the assessment developers themselves. If the confidence band around the score is too broad, it serves as a cautionary flag that something should be done.

Since assessment on speaking tests is often criterion-referenced, reliability coefficients and the SEM are only partially appropriate for them (Brown and Hudson, 2002). As an extreme example, if an end-of-course speaking test was rated on a criterion-referenced scale of 5 levels and the teaching and learning on the course were successful, most of the students would achieve high scores. This would result in low traditional reliability estimates, because the calculation of these statistics starts from the expectation that the examinees should be spread along the scale. If the range of student scores is small because of successful learning, the test developers should use other means for estimating reliability. Cross-tabulation, for example, might reveal a high degree of exact agreement, which indicates that the scoring is reliable.

There are also more complex statistical procedures for estimating score reliability. For example, a range of statistics can be calculated to express the degree of agreement in a cross-tabulation (see e.g. Brown and Hudson, 2002). Moreover, generalisability theory (Shavelson and Webb, 1981; Bachman, forthcoming) can be used to analyse the causes of error variation in the scores, whether it is tasks, raters, or some interaction between them, for example. Multi-faceted item response theory (Linacre, 1989; McNamara, 1996) can be used to put scales, raters, tasks and examinees on the same measurement scale and investigate their quality. However, these analyses tend to require large amounts of data and a fair amount of statistical expertise. For this reason, they are usually only used with formal speaking tests where the number of participants allows such analyses. In score user manuals, the reliability indices that these more advanced methods deliver are often explained with reference to the traditional concept of reliability as discussed above. Introductions to the methods and references for further study can be found in most educational measurement textbooks.

Defining validity for speaking assessments

Validity is the most important consideration in test development. In short, it refers to the meaningfulness of the scores, which defines a broad scope of concerns. Regarding tasks and criteria, one of the main concerns is content coverage and comprehensiveness in relation to the definition of the test purpose. Another important area is correspondence between the test and the non-test activities that the scores are expected to reflect. Validity concerns also include the impact of the test on the examinees and score users.

Whereas it was possible to specify aspects of reliability that are particularly relevant for speaking assessments, validity is such a fundamental quality that it is not possible to highlight particular aspects of it that would be more relevant for speaking than others. However, this does not mean that validity is an abstract theoretical concern. Rather, it is a practical quality that is part of all test development work. All the procedures of test development that have been discussed in this book provide evidence for a validity argument about the scores.

Ensuring the validity of speaking scores

The validity of speaking scores is grounded in the purpose that the scores are intended to serve, such as certifying a health professional's ability to serve patients in the official language of their new country or giving learners feedback about their speaking skills to help them learn more. Spending some time on specifying the purpose of the test when the development is first started helps the developers set the scene for validation work. Next, the developers should attempt to define, as clearly as possible, what kind of speaking their test is intended to assess.

In this book, I have talked about three approaches to defining the speaking construct for assessment. The linguistic approach focuses on language forms. Task demands and performance qualities are seen in terms of vocabulary, grammar, pronunciation and fluency, regardless of what it is that the speakers are asked to do with language. The communicative approach focuses on the activities that the examinees are asked to do, and the performances are assessed according to how well the examinees can use the skills and strategies that the activity requires. They may also be assessed in terms of linguistic criteria, but communication criteria make better use of the information that the tasks are designed to reveal. The task-based approach defines the skills assessed in terms of the situations and roles simulated in the test, and expresses scores in terms of the examinees' ability to deal with the tasks that were included. This approach is typical for specific purpose testing, but it can also be applied in generic purpose speaking tests whenever a task can be identified clearly enough. Tasks that are appropriate for task-based assessment evoke the situation, speaker roles, and purposes of the event simply by their names. A doctor's consultation is a possible task-based assessment task. A description is not; descriptions form part of many different speech events, and if they are important for testing the developers are better off defining the tasks and criteria in terms of description as a communication activity.

After the purpose of the test has been clarified and the test construct defined, the next step in validation is showing evidence from the test

development process that the tasks and criteria, as well as the administration and rating procedures, actually implement the construct. This
starts from using the task specifications to characterise the tasks. Next,
the developers should explain the relevance of the tasks to the purpose,
and the degree to which they are representative of the possible tasks that
this purpose might include. They can also show that the tasks and task
materials are authentic or that they engage the examinees in spoken
interaction in similar ways to the non-test situation that the test is
intended to be relevant to. Moreover, they can show that any features of
the test situation that are not relevant to the target-language-use situation are minimal and do not influence the scores to any significant degree.

The next step is the evaluation of the rating criteria. First of all, these
must be coherent with the purpose of the test, the construct definition,
and the tasks, which the developers can show by comparing the definitions. Secondly, they must be defined concretely to make them easy to
use, which can be shown for example by different drafts of the criteria if
they have been modified as a result of trials and rater comments, comparisons between the criteria and transcribed performances, and rater
evaluations of the scales.

The test administration and scoring processes can be evaluated in terms
of their consistency and their coherence with the construct definition.
Data for this can include administration and scoring plans or manuals,
administrator and rater reports, interlocutor and rater training materials
and evidence about the qualification of the selected interlocutors and
raters, and all reliability monitoring data that the developers have. This is
the point where reliability and validity are most clearly interrelated.

Finally, validation evidence includes all the planning and monitoring
that the test developers do related to score use. In addition to administrative records, the developers can study the examinee attitudes to and
experiences with the test, the **washback effect** or the effect of the test on
teaching and teacher or learner attitudes towards learning and the test,
and other actual consequences of score use. For a detailed discussion of
approaches to validation, see Bachman (forthcoming).

Future directions in assessing speaking

In response to increased pressure for administrative accountability, both
formal and informal speaking assessments have become more frequent
in recent years. This has increased the range of different speaking assess-

ment procedures that test developers can choose from, but it also high-lights the need for an increasing number of test developers and users to know more about speaking assessment. In this section, I will look into the future of speaking assessment to identify some promising areas of development and discuss issues that will need to be addressed. I will start from promising areas of development and continue with unresolved problems.

Communication-oriented tasks and criteria

Communication-oriented tasks focus on examinees' skills to structure information effectively and communicate smoothly in a socially accept-able manner. These have been used in speaking tests for a long time, but communication-oriented criteria are quite new. To create them, assessment developers need to observe learner performances on the tasks and specify what it is that makes them more or less successful from the perspective of reaching the task goals. In information-related talk such as narratives or explanations, success partly depends on the content and sequencing of the examinees' talk. Another part has to do with how the examinees deliver the information: how fluent and accurate they are, what strategies they use to keep the interaction going and get their message across, and how well they take the listener into account. Scales for evaluating these skills need to be developed and tried out. Evaluation of their usefulness will help not only the development of speaking assessments but also teaching curricula and materials.

Pair and group tasks

Speaking assessments are time-consuming to administer and rate. Sometimes the administration may be speeded up by using tape-based tests, but rating still takes time, as the raters have to listen to the perfor-mances second by second. One way of making efficient use of testing and scoring time in live tests is to have two or more examinees interact with each other. This puts the examinees in an equal power position in rela-tion to each other, and this affects many different aspects of their talk. In many senses, peer interaction makes communication in the test more realistic than the kind of interaction that is possible between an interloc-utor and an examinee, but it also brings disadvantages. Most evidently, the developers need to turn over some of the control of the test discourse to the examinees, which means that the responsibility for showing their own and their peers' language skills is in their hands.

The challenge with pair and group tasks for the future is finding the types of tasks that are most appropriate for pair and small group testing. Furthermore, experiments will need to be conducted to find the most efficient ways of giving task instructions and presenting task materials in ways that support the test discourse while not making it artificial. The benefits and drawbacks of different picture-based or text-based materials will need to be investigated. Similarly, the appropriateness of information gap tasks for examinees of varying ages and ability levels will need to be studied.

Pair and group tasks are already being used in many settings, so the main developments related to them are not about learning the basic rules for writing them but about how to make them more effective. The key is observing learner performances and analysing the strengths and weaknesses of different task features in particular assessment contexts. Further development of rating procedures for group tasks is also needed. Since rating needs to be fair, we need to know, for example, how many examinees a rater can observe in one interaction. The studies can be based on a combination of observation, self-reflection and score analysis.

Rating checklists

The flexibility of rating checklists makes them a promising tool for assessing speaking especially in learning-related settings. They allow raters to note down comments about the unique features of different performances quickly. The criteria are usually grouped in a way that makes conceptual sense for raters, and the same grouping can also be used when giving feedback to the examinees. Since rating checklists are a relatively new tool in speaking assessment, the questions about them are basic, such as finding the most promising strategies for creating useful descriptors for checklists and evaluating the comprehensiveness of a draft checklist.

Ultimately, rating checklists are only going to become more frequent if the information that they provide is actually interesting or useful for the examinees. When trying out checklists, this is an important point to evaluate.

Peer evaluation

Another promising area in speaking assessment is peer evaluation. The motivation for peer evaluation in educational settings is more than making students attend to what is going on in the classroom when they are not communicating themselves, although that is one of the advantages. It can help learners become more aware of their learning goals, learn through evaluation, and learn from each other. Peer evaluation is not a panacea, however. It can supplement teacher-based evaluation but it cannot replace it. Teachers provide a different perspective to student performances because they are specialists in language learning and they know the goals of the curriculum. Nevertheless, peer evaluation is useful because it allows teachers to share some of the rating responsibility with their students, and it is especially useful in speaking assessment, which is time-consuming if rated by one person only.

There are some challenges with peer evaluation as well, however. The main one is defining the criteria so that the learners can use them. Linguistic criteria may not be suitable, because students are not as adept at language analysis as teachers or raters, whereas task-related criteria may prove more effective. It is a good idea to develop the criteria for peer evaluation together with the learners. Discussions about the features of good performances on specific tasks can clarify the learning goals for both teachers and students.

Feedback

Informal feedback about speaking skills is very common in teaching contexts, but more organised strategies for reporting feedback to learners also need to be developed. Useful feedback is concrete and descriptive, and it relates examinee performances to goals or descriptions of good performance. Evaluative comments like 'good job' are insufficient as feedback, because they do not tell learners about what they did well, or what they might do better. Feedback that can do this helps build close links between assessment and teaching.

One possibility for developing more structured feedback mechanisms for speaking assessment is using rating checklists. However, the usefulness of this type of feedback for learners will need to be evaluated empirically. Organising feedback reports in terms of course learning goals is also a possibility, but this means that the teachers would need to be able to define the speaking goals of a course concretely enough to allow this. Moreover, the level of student achievement of the goals at different stages of the course would need to be stated in terms of some kind of generic or goal-related scale. This needs to be developed and tried out in order to evaluate the usefulness of this form of feedback in practical terms.

Unanswered questions

Much of the current research in assessing speaking deals with formal proficiency tests. In the past few decades, the main topics have been the nature of the individual interview as a testing technique, differences in test and task types, task difficulty, interlocutor behaviour, and the rating process. The features of examinee speech, especially fluency, have also been studied. With the increase of learning-related and informal assessments, more studies will need to be conducted into the tasks and testing processes that are relevant to that context. These may look quite different from the existing studies on speaking assessment, because the questions will arise from the learning context. Some of the studies may focus on the assessment format, such as self-assessment, peer evaluation, or the integration of the speaking assessment with other skills, while others may study the effects of surprise content or topics versus practised functions and topics, the use of different kinds of pictures versus verbal task materials, the effects of language choice in the task materials, or the amount of instruction and task structuring that are needed with different kinds of learning-related speaking assessment.

In pair or group tasks, or even when an examinee interacts with an interlocutor, the performance of one speaker is likely to affect the performance of the other(s). In discourse analysis, this is discussed under the heading of co-construction of meaning. What we need to understand better is exactly how one person's performance affects the other's. We also need to know what it is about an examinee's talk and his or her accommodation to the conversation partner that should be appreciated in order to make evaluations in a fair way. Tests sometimes use a criterion such as 'discourse skills' to evaluate this, but the scale descriptors are usually rather vague, and they concentrate on a rater's perception of the flow of the conversation. This needs to be supplemented or replaced by descriptions of what the examinees actually say and do. The patterns that make a difference are likely to include recycling of phrases and structures from previous turns and the explicit and implicit development of themes and topics between speakers. However, only concrete analyses of test perfor-mances combined with ratings of discourse competence can provide accurate detailed descriptions of this. The analyses can start from listen-ing to recordings of some pair or group interactions and comparing the examinees' talk with phrases used in the draft criteria. If the relationship between the performances and the criteria is not straightforward, a more focused listening-based analysis can support the next step of develop-ment. More extensive analyses, possibly based on transcribed perfor-mances, can then follow if the developers have time and interest for that.

Another area that we need to understand better is the usefulness of task-specific scales. We need to learn when it is useful to use them, how best to develop them, and how to evaluate their generalisability. Task-specific scales are used especially in specific purpose assessment, where the scores help make practical, often work-related decisions, but they are also sometimes used in generic-purpose assessment. Especially in these contexts, we need to learn when to use them. This can be studied by using two different types of scale to assess a single set of taped performances on a few tasks.

The way forward

The way forward in speaking assessment is through action, reflection and reporting. We can learn more about assessing speaking by arranging tests and analysing what we are doing while developing, administering and using them. Speaking assessments are time-consuming and they require a fair amount of work. By analysing the starting situation where the scores are needed and by evaluating what we are doing, we can get the most out of the effort that is spent on it. Although reporting on what we are doing means spending more time still, it is also helpful because it forces us to think about the activities more carefully. Conversely, learning about other speaking testers' experiences can help us learn more. This expanding cycle of knowledge helps us develop better speaking assessments and moves the field of assessing speaking forward.

References

ACTFL (1999). *The ACTFL Proficiency Guidelines: Speaking (revised 1999).* Yonkers, NY: ACTFL.

AERA, APA and NCME (1999). *Standards for Educational and Psychological Testing.* American Educational Research Association, American Psychological Association, National Council on Measurement in Education. Washington DC: American Educational Research Association.

Alderson, J. C. (1991). Bands and scores. In J. C. Alderson and B. North (eds), *Language Testing in the 1990s.* London: Macmillan, pp. 71–86.

Alderson, J. C., Clapham, C. and Wall, D. (1995). *Language Test Construction and Evaluation.* Cambridge: CUP.

Austin, J. L. (1962). *How To Do Things With Words.* Oxford: OUP.

Bachman, L.F. (1988). Problems in examining the validity of the ACTFL oral proficiency interview. *Studies in Second Language Acquisition* 10 (2), 149–164.

Bachman, L. F. (1990). *Fundamental Considerations in Language Testing.* Oxford: OUP.

Bachman, L. F. (2002). Some reflections on task-based language performance assessment. *Language Testing* 19 (4), 453–476.

Bachman, L. F. (forthcoming). *Statistical Analyses in Language Assessment.* Cambridge: CUP.

Bachman, L. F. and Palmer, A. (1996). *Language Testing in Practice.* Oxford: OUP.

Bachman, L. F. and Savignon, S. J. (1986). The evaluation of communicative language proficiency: a critique of the ACTFL oral interview. *The Modern Language Journal* 70 (4), 380–390.

Bardovi-Harlig, K. (1999). Exploring the interlanguage of interlanguage pragmatics: a research agenda for acquisitional pragmatics. *Language Learning* 49, 677–713.

Berry, V. (1997). Gender and personality as factors of interlocutor variability in oral performance tests. Paper presented at the Language Testing Research Colloquium in Orlando, FL.

Bialystok, E. (1991). Achieving proficiency in a second language: a processing description. In R. Phillipson, E. Kellerman, L. Selinker, M. Sharwood Smith and M. Swain (eds), *Foreign/Second Language Pedagogy Research*. Clevedon: Multilingual Matters, pp. 63–78.

Brindley, G. (1998). Describing language development? Rating scales and SLA. In L. F. Bachman and A. D. Cohen (eds), *Interfaces between Second Language Acquisition and Language Testing Research*. Cambridge: CUP, pp. 112–140.

Brown, A. (1993). The role of test-taker feedback in the development of an occupational language proficiency test. *Language Testing* 10 (3), 277–303.

Brown, A. (2000). An investigation of the rating process in the IELTS Speaking Module. In R. Tulloh (ed.), *IELTS Research Reports 1999, Vol. 3*. Sydney: ELICOS, pp. 49–85.

Brown, A. (2003). Interviewer variation and the co-construction of speaking proficiency. *Language Testing* 20, 1–25.

Brown, A. and Hill, K. (1998). Interviewer style and candidate performance in the IELTS Oral Interview. In S. Woods (ed.), *IELTS Research Reports 1997*, Volume 1. Sydney: ELICOS, pp. 173–191.

Brown, A. and Lumley, T. (1997). Interviewer variability in specific-purpose language performance tests. In V. Kohonen, A. Huhta, L. Kurki-Suonio and S. Luoma (eds), *Current Developments and Alternatives in Language Assessment: proceedings of LTRC 1996*. Jyväskylä: University of Jyväskylä and University of Tampere, pp. 137–150.

Brown, A., McNamara, T., Iwashita, N. and O'Hagan, S. (2001). *Investigating Raters' Orientations in Specific-purpose Task-based Oral Assessment*. TOEFL 2000 Research and Development project report. Submitted June 2001.

Brown, G. (1989). Making sense: the interaction of linguistic expression and contextual information. *Applied Linguistics* 10 (1), 97–109.

Brown, G. (1996). Language learning, competence and performance. In G. Brown, K. Malmkjaer and J. Williams (eds), *Performance and Competence in Second Language Acquisition*, pp. 187–203. Cambridge: CUP.

Brown, G., Anderson, A., Shillcock, R. and Yule, G. (1984). *Teaching Talk: Strategies for production and assessment*. Cambridge: CUP.

Brown, G. and Yule, G. (1983). *Teaching the Spoken Language: an approach based on the analysis of conversational English*. Cambridge: CUP.

Brown, J. D. and Hudson, T. (2002). *Criterion-referenced Language Testing*. Cambridge: CUP.

Brown, P. and Levinson, S. C. (1987). *Politeness: Some universals in language usage*. Cambridge: CUP.

Butler, B. (1985). *Statistics in Linguistics*. New York: Blackwell.

Bygate, M. (1987). *Speaking*. Oxford: OUP.

CAEL (2000). *Test takers' Preparation Guide.* Ottawa: Carleton University. Document available online at www.carleton.ca/slals/cael.htm.

CAEL (2002). *Canadian Academic English Language Assessment.* Website available on the Internet at www.carleton.ca/slals/cael.htm.

Canale, M. and Swain, M. (1980). Theoretical bases of communicative approaches to second language teaching and testing. *Applied Linguistics* 1, 1–47.

Carter, R. and McCarthy, M. (1995). Grammar and the spoken language. *Applied Linguistics*, 16, 141–158.

Carter, R. and McCarthy, M. (1997). *Exploring Spoken English.* Cambridge: CUP.

Chafe, W. (1985). Linguistic differences produced by differences between speech and writing. In D. R. Olsen, N. Torrance and A. Hilyard (eds), *Literacy and Language Learning: the nature and consequences of reading and writing.* Cambridge: CUP.

Chalhoub-Deville, M. (1995). A contextualised approach to describing oral proficiency. *Language Learning* 45, 251–281.

Channell, J. (1994). *Vague Language.* Cambridge: CUP.

Chapelle, C., Grabe, W. and Berns, M. (1997). *Communicative Language Proficiency: Definition and implications for TOEFL 2000.* TOEFL Monograph Series 10. Princeton, NJ: Educational Testing Service.

Clark, J. L. D. and Clifford, R. T. (1988). The FSI/ILR/ACTFL proficiency scales and testing techniques: development, current status and needed research. *Studies in Second Language Acquisition* 10, 129–147.

Council of Europe (2001). *Common European Framework of Reference for Languages: Learning, teaching, assessment.* Cambridge: CUP.

Cronbach, L. J. (1990). *Essentials of Psychological Testing.* Fifth edition. New York: Harper and Row.

Douglas, D. (1998). Testing methods in context-based second language research. In L. F. Bachman and A. D. Cohen (eds), *Interfaces between Second Language Acquisition and Language Testing Research.* Cambridge: CUP, pp. 141–155.

Douglas, D. (2000). *Assessing Language for Specific Purposes: Theory and practice.* Cambridge: CUP.

Douglas, D. and Smith, J. (1997). *Theoretical Underpinnings of the Test of Spoken English Revision Project.* TOEFL Monograph Series 9. Princeton, NJ: Educational Testing Service.

Educational Testing Service (2002). *Test of Spoken English.* Website available on the Internet at http://www.toefl.org/tse/tseindx.html.

Ek, J. A. van (1975). *The Threshold Level in a European Unit/Credit System for Modern Language Learning by Adults.* Strasbourg: Council of Europe. (Republished in 1977 as *The Threshold Level for Modern Language Learning.* London: Longman.)

Elder, C., Iwashita, N. and McNamara, T. (2002). Estimating the difficulty of oral proficiency tasks: what does the test-taker have to offer? *Language Testing* 19 (4), 337–346.

Ellis, N. (2002). Frequency effects in language processing: a review with implications for theories of implicit and explicit language acquisition. *Studies in Second Language Acquisition* 24, 143–188.

Ellis, R. (1989). Are classroom and naturalistic acquisition the same? A study of the classroom acquisition of German word order rules. *Studies in Second Language Acquisition* 11, 305–328.

Esser, U. (1995). *Oral Language Testing: the concept of fluency revisited.* MA dissertation, Lancaster University, Lancaster, UK.

ETS (2001a). *Information Bulletin for the Test of Spoken English.* TSE 2001–02. Princeton, NJ: Educational Testing Service. Online version of a current bulletin available from http://www.toefl.org/tse/tseindx.html.

ETS (2001b). TSE and SPEAK score user guide. 2001–2992 edition. Princeton, NJ: Educational Testing Service. Online version of a current score user guide available from http://www.toefl.org/tse/tseindx.html.

ETS (2002). *TSE Practice Questions.* Downloaded from http://www.toefl.org/tse/tseindx.html under the Practice questions link, 15 May 2002.

Faerch, C. and Kasper, G. (1983). *Strategies in Interlanguage Communication.* London: Longman.

Foster, P. and Skehan, P. (1996). The influence of planning and task type on second language performance. *Studies in Second Language Acquisition* 18, 299–323.

Fox, J. (2001). *It's all about Meaning: L2 test validation in and through the landscape of an evolving construct.* PhD thesis, McGill University, Montreal, CA.

Fox, J., Pychyl, T. and Zumbo, B. (1993). Psychometric properties of the CAEL Assessment, I: an overview of development, format, and scoring procedures. In Fox (ed.), *Carleton Papers in Applied Language Studies,* Volume X. Ottawa: Centre for Applied Language Studies, Carleton University.

Freed, B. (1995). What makes us think that students who study abroad become fluent? In B. Freed (ed.), *Second Language Acquisition in a Study Abroad Context.* Amsterdam: John Benjamins.

Fulcher, G. (1993). *The Construction and Validation of Rating Scales for Oral Tests in English as a Foreign Language.* Unpublished PhD thesis, Lancaster University, Lancaster, UK.

Fulcher, G. (1996). Does thick description lead to smart tests? A data-based approach to rating scale construction. *Language Testing* 13 (2), 208–238.

Fulcher, G. (1997). The testing of speaking in a second language. In C. Clapham and D. Corson (eds), *Language Testing and Assessment, Vol. 7 of the Encyclopedia of Language Education.* Dordrecht: Kluwer Academic Publishers, pp. 75–85.

Grice, H. P. (1975). Logic in conversation. In P. Cole and J. L. Morgan (eds), *Syntax and Semantics,* Vol. 3: Speech Acts. New York: Academic Press, pp. 41–58.

Grove, E. and Brown, A. (2001). Tasks and criteria in a test of oral communication skills for first-year health science students. *Melbourne Papers in Language Testing* 10 (1), pp. 37–47.

Halliday, M. A. K. (1976). The form of a functional grammar. In G. Kress (ed.), *Halliday: System and function in language*. Oxford: OUP.

Hasselgren, A. (1998). *Smallwords and Valid Testing*. PhD thesis. Department of English, University of Bergen, Bergen, Norway.

Heaton, J. B. (1991). *Writing English Language Tests*. Fourth impression. London: Longman.

Henning, G. (1987). *A Guide to Language Testing*. Cambridge, Mass: Newbury House.

House, J. (1996). Developing pragmatic fluency in English as a foreign language: Routines and metapragmatic awareness. *Studies in Second Language Acquisition* 18, 225–252.

Hymes, D. (1971). Competence and performance in linguistic theory. In R. Huxley and E. Ingram (eds), *Language Acquisition: Models and methods*. London: Academic Press, pp. 3–24.

Hymes, D. (1972). On communicative competence. In J. B. Pride and J. Holmes (eds), *Sociolinguistics*. Harmondsworth: Penguin, pp. 269–293.

Iwashita, N. (1999). The validity of the paired interview format in oral performance assessment. *Melbourne Papers in Language Testing* 8 (1), 51–66.

Jamieson, J., Jones, S., Kirsch, I., Mosenthal, P. and Taylor, C. (2000). *TOEFL 2000 Framework: a working paper*. TOEFL Monograph Series 16. Princeton, NJ: Educational Testing Service.

Jones, R. (2001). A consciousness-raising approach to the teaching of conversational storytelling skills. *ELT Journal* 55, 155–63.

Kärkkäinen, E. (1992). Modality as a strategy in interaction: epistemic modality in the language of native and non-native speakers of English. In L. Bouton and Y. Kachru (eds), *Pragmatics and Language Learning*, Vol. 3, Division of English as an international language. University of Illinois at Urbana-Champaign, pp. 197–216.

Kasper, G. (1996). Introduction: interlanguage pragmatics in SLA. *Studies in Second Language Acquisition* 18, 145–148.

Kasper, G. (2001). Four perspectives on L2 pragmatic development. *Applied Linguistics* 22 (4), 502–530.

Koponen, M. (1995). Let your language and thoughts flow! Is there a case for 'fluency' in ELT and applied linguistics? Paper presented at the Language Testing Forum, Newcastle, UK, November 1995.

Kramsch, C. (1986). From language proficiency to interactional competence. *The Modern Language Journal* 70 (4), 366–372.

Lantolf, J. P. (2000). Introducing sociocultural theory. In J. P. Lantolf (ed.), *Sociocultural Theory and Second Language Learning*. Oxford: OUP, pp. 1–26.

Lantolf, J. P. and Frawley, W. (1985). Oral proficiency testing: a critical analysis. *The Modern Language Journal* 69, 337–345.

Lantolf, J. and Pavlenko, A. (1998). (S)econd (L)anguage (A)ctivity theory: understanding second language learners as people. In M. Breen (ed.), *Learner Con-*

tributions to Language Learning: New directions in research. Harlow, Essex: Pearson Education Limited, pp. 141–158.

Larsen-Freeman, D. and Long, M. (1991). *An Introduction to Second Language Acquisition Research.* London: Longman.

Lazaraton, A. (1992). The structural organization of a language interview: a conversation analytic perspective, *System* 20, 373–386.

Leather, J. and James, A. (1996). Second language speech. In William C. Ritchie and Tej K. Bhatia (eds), *Handbook of Second Language Acquisition.* San Diego, CA: Academic Press, pp. 269–316.

Lennon, P. (1990). Investigating fluency in EFL: a quantitative approach. *Language Learning* 40 (3), 387–417.

Lier, L. van (1989). Reeling, writhing, drawling, stretching and fainting in coils: oral proficiency interviews as conversation. *TESOL Quarterly* 23, 489–503.

Linacre, M. (1989). *Many-faceted Rasch measurement.* Chicago, IL: MESA Press.

Linn, R. and Gronlund, N. (1995). *Measurement and Assessment in Teaching* (seventh edition). Englewood Cliffs. NJ.: Merrill.

Lynch, B. and Davidson, F. (1994). Criterion-referenced language test development: linking curricula, teachers, and tests. *TESOL Quarterly* 28 (4), 727–743.

Lynch, T. (2001) Seeing what they meant: transcribing as a route to noticing. *ELT Journal* 55 (2), 124–132.

McCarthy, M. and Carter, R. (1995). Spoken grammar: what is it and how can we teach it? *ELT Journal* 49, 207–218.

McCarthy, M., and Carter, R. (1997). *Language as discourse: Perspectives for language teaching.* London: Longman.

McDowell, C. (1995). Assessing the language proficiency of overseas-qualified teachers: the English language skills assessment (ELSA). In G. Brindley (ed.) *Language Assessment in Action.* Sydney: NCELTR, Macquarie University, pp. 11–29.

McKay, P. (1995). Developing ESL proficiency descriptions for the school context: the NLLIA bandscales. In G. Brindley (ed.) *Language Assessment in Action.* Sydney: NCELTR, Macquarie University, pp. 31–63.

McNamara, T. (1996). *Measuring Second Language Performance.* London: Longman.

McNamara, T. (1997). 'Interaction' in second language performance assessment: whose performance? *Applied Linguistics* 18, 446–466.

Milanovic, M., Saville, N., Pollitt, A. and Cook, A. (1996). Developing rating scales for CASE: theoretical concerns and analyses. In A. Cumming and R. Berwick (eds), *Validation in Language Testing.* Clevedon, Avon: Multimedia Matters, pp. 15–38.

Morley, J. (1991). The pronunciation component in teaching English to speakers of other languages. *TESOL Quarterly* 25, 481–520.

Nasjonalt læremiddelsenter (Norway) (1996). Kartleggning av kommunikativ kompetanse i engelsk. Speaking test. 8th class. Oslo: Nasjonalt læremiddelsenter.

National Board of Education (2002). *The Framework of the Finnish National Certificates.* Helsinki: National Board of Education.

National Certificates (2003). *Testiesite. Englannin kieli, ylin taso. Jyväskylä.* Centre for Applied Language Studies, University of Jyväskylä. Manuscript of a test brochure.

Nattinger, J. and DeCarrico, J. (1992). *Lexical Phrases and Language Teaching.* Oxford: OUP.

Nikula, T. (1996). *Pragmatic Force Modifiers: a study in interlanguage pragmatics.* PhD thesis, Department of English, University of Jyväskylä, Jyväskylä, FI.

Norris, J. M. (2002). Interpretations, intended uses and designs in task-based language assessment. Editorial in *Language Testing* 19, 337–346.

Norris, J. M., Brown, J. D., Hudson, T. D. and Bonk, W. (2000). Assessing performance on complex L2 tasks: investigating raters, examinees, and tasks. Paper presented at the 22nd Language Testing Research Colloquium, Vancouver, British Columbia, Canada.

Norris, J. M., Brown, J. D., Hudson, T. D. and Bonk, W. (2002). Examinee abilities and task difficulty in task-based second language performance assessment. *Language Testing* 19, 395–418.

North, B. (1996/2000). *The Development of a Common Framework Scale of Language Proficiency.* PhD thesis, Thames Valley University, London, UK. Published in 2000 as *The Development of a Common Framework Scale of Language Proficiency.* New York: Peter Lang.

Nunan, D. (1989). *Designing Tasks for the Communicative Classroom.* Cambridge: CUP.

Nunan, D. (1993). Task-based syllabus design: selecting, grading and sequencing tasks. In G. Crookes and S. Gass (eds), *Tasks in a Pedagogical Context: Integrating theory and practice.* Clevedon: Multilingual Matters, pp. 55–68.

O'Loughlin, K. (2001). The equivalence of direct and semi-direct speaking tests. *Studies in Language Testing* 13. Cambridge: CUP.

O'Sullivan, B. (2002). Learner acquaintanceship and OPT pair-task performance. *Language Testing* 19, 277–295.

Ochs, E. (1979). Transcription as theory. In E. Ochs and B. Schiefferlin (eds), *Developmental Pragmatics.* New York: Academic Press, pp. 43–72.

Ordinate (2002). PhonePass sample test. Available from http://www.ordinate.com under the 'Try PhonePass' link.

Pawley, A. and Syder, F. H. (1983). Two puzzles for linguistic theory: nativelike selection and nativelike fluency. In J. C. Richards and R. W. Schmidt (eds), *Language and Communication.* London: Longman.

Pennington, M. C. and Richards, J. C. (1986). Pronunciation revisited. *TESOL Quarterly* 20, 207–225.

Pienemann, M. (1998). *Language Processing and Second Language Development: Processability theory.* Amsterdam: Benjamins.

Pollitt, A. and Murray, N. (1996). What raters really pay attention to. In M. Milanovic and N. Saville (eds), *Performance Testing, Cognition and Assessment. Selected papers from the 15ᵗʰ Language Testing Research Colloquium, Cambridge and Arnhem.* Cambridge: CUP, pp. 74–91.

Popham, W. J. (1990). *Modern Educational Measurement* (second edition). Englewood Cliffs, NJ: Prentice-Hall.

Proficiency Standards Division (1999). *OPI 2000 Tester Certification Workshop.* Monterey: Defense Language Institute Foreign Language Center.

Purpura, J. (forthcoming). *Assessing Grammar.* Cambridge: CUP.

Quirk, R. and Greenbaum, S. (1976). *A University Grammar of English.* Fifth impression. London: Longman.

Read, J. (2000). *Assessing Vocabulary.* Cambridge: CUP.

Reves, T. (1991). From testing research to educational policy: a comprehensive test of oral proficiency. In J. C. Alderson and B. North (eds), *Language Testing in the 1990s.* London: Modern English Publications and the British Council, pp. 178–188.

Rintell, E. M. (1990). That's incredible: stories of emotions told by second language learners and native speakers. In R. C. Scarcella, E. S. Anderson, and S. D. Krashen (eds), *Developing Communicative Competence in a Second Language.* New York: Newbury House.

Robinson, P. (1995). Task complexity and second language narrative discourse. *Language Learning* 45, 99–140.

Robinson, P. (2001). Task complexity, task difficulty and task production: exploring interactions in a componential framework. *Applied Linguistics* 22, 27–57.

Salsbury, T. and Bardovi-Harlig, K. (2000). Oppositional talk and the acquisition of modality in L2 English. In B. Swiertzbin, F. Morris, M. Anderson, C. A. Klee and E. Tarone (eds), *Social and Cognitive Factors in Second Language Acquisition.* Sommerville, MA: Cascadilla Press, pp. 56–76.

Savignon, S. (1985). Evaluation of communicative competence: the ACTFL provisional proficiency guidelines. *The Modern Language Journal* 69, 129–134.

Schiffrin, D. (1994). *Approaches to Discourse.* Oxford: Blackwell.

Shavelson, R. J. and Webb, N. M. (1981). *Generalizability Theory: a primer.* Newbury Park, CA: Sage Publications.

Shohamy, E. (1994). The validity of direct versus semi-direct oral tests. *Language Testing* 11, 99–123.

Shohamy, E., Reves, T. and Bejarano, Y. (1986). Introducing a new comprehensive test of oral proficiency. *English Language Teaching Journal* 40, 212–220.

Skehan, P. and Foster, P. (1997). The influence of planning and post-task activities on accuracy and complexity in task-based learning. *Language Teaching Research* 1, 185–212.

Skehan, P. and Foster, P. (2001). Cognition and tasks. In P. Robinson (ed.), *Cognition and Second Language Instruction.* Cambridge: CUP.

Stansfield, C. W. and Kenyon, D. M. (1991). *Development of the Texas Oral Proficiency Test (TOPT): Final Report.*

Swain, M. (2001). Examining dialogue: another approach to content specification and to validating inferences drawn from test scores. *Language Testing* 18 (3), 275–302.

Tannen, D. (1982). Oral and literate strategies in spoken and written discourse. *Language* 58, 1–20.

Thomas, J. 1995. *Meaning in Interaction. An introduction to pragmatics.* London: Longman.

Towell, R., Hawkins, R. and Bazergui, N. (1996). The development of fluency in advanced learners of French. *Applied Linguistics* 17, 84–119.

UCLES (2001a). *First Certificate Handbook.* Available online from http://www.cambridgeesol.org/support/dloads/

UCLES (2001b). Certificate in Advanced English Handbook. Available online from http://www.cambridgee-sol.org/support/dloads/cae/cae_hb_samp_p5_faq.pdf

UCLES (2001c). *Business English Certificate Handbook.* Available online from http://www.cambridgeesol.org/support/dloads/

Weir, C. (1993). *Understanding and Developing Language Tests.* New York: Prentice Hall.

Wiggins, G. (1998). *Educative Assessment.* San Francisco: Jossey-Bass.

Wigglesworth, G. (1997). An investigation of planning time and proficiency level on oral test discourse. *Language Testing* 14 (1), 85–106.

Wigglesworth, G. and O'Loughlin, K. (1993). An investigation into the comparability of direct and semi-direct versions of an oral interaction test in English. *Melbourne Papers in Language Testing* 2 (1), 56–67.

Wilkins, D. A. (1976). *Notional Syllabuses.* Oxford: OUP.

Index